When God Speaks to My Heart

A Daybook of
Personal Moments with God

[handwritten inscription:] To Linda, may these words of love and encouragement from God's heart bring you great joy as He speaks to your heart. With blessings, Rosalie Willis Storment

Rosalie Willis

WHITE STONE BOOKS

LAKELAND, FLORIDA

09 08 07 06 05 / 10 9 8 6 7 5 4 3 2 1

When God Speaks to My Heart —
A Daybook of Personal Moments with God
ISBN 1-59379-042-2
Copyright © 2005 by Rosalie Willis
P.O. Box 324
Post Falls, Idaho 83877-0324

Published by White Stone Books
P.O. Box 2835
Lakeland, Florida 33806

Dedication

"Heart Friends," who pray for us with love, are one of the most valuable gifts we can receive from God in this adventure of life. He has honored and blessed me with many "Heart Friends" near and far, around the block and around the world, who hold my arms up with love and prayer. It is to these precious "Heart Friends" that I dedicate this "Book of Love from God."

Introduction

I was blessed to be raised in a Godly home, and always knew God as a loving compassionate Father. A Father I loved with all my heart.

But it wasn't until the early 70's, when I became captivated by a certain Scripture, "Pray Without Ceasing," that my life became wonderfully changed forever! At that point, I determined in my heart that I would strive to include Him in every thought and word, so that every contemplation and statement might be a prayer to Him. Shortly after I made that decision, I discovered that God was not only pleased by my decision, but He also wanted to speak to my heart.

What joy to learn that God actually created us for loving fellowship and longs to speak to us in return!

God didn't create prayer to be a one-way monologue, but instead a pathway to enter into intimate fellowship with Him. God has given each of us the ability to hear His voice. But through fear or doubt we often hesitate and question what we are hearing as simply our own thoughts, or we even distrust the origin of what we sense we are hearing.

When approached or questioned by those seeking to hear from God, I always respond that His words are continually filled with beauty, peace, hope, encouragement, love, joy, and wisdom—causing us to know how precious we are to Him, and how much He loves us. Even words of correction from God bring hope and encouragement.

When God began speaking to my heart, I set in motion writing down every word He spoke. Each word a treasure, never to be forgotten. Every day I would sit in His Presence and say, *"Father, what is on Your heart for me to know today?"* Day-by-day, year-by-year, He would share with me His love and plans for my life and for the lives of those I loved.

After initially discovering that it was possible to hear His voice, one of the first things I ever asked God was, *"What am I doing with the raising of my daughter that I should not be doing, and what should I be doing that I am not?"* He responded, *"I am raising her to be the strong tall oak of the forest, a blessing to many,"* and, of course, that is what she beautifully became!

Everything I am living out today is a result of many promises given by God as He has spoken to my heart through the last 30 years.

Seven years ago my carotid artery collapsed, tore, and was disintegrating, causing me to have strokes. After three Code Blues, ten hours of surgery, and a month in the hospital, the doctors didn't expect me to live. But I knew I would not only live, but I would be completely healed. Why? Because the last word God had spoken to my heart—before entering the hospital—was a promise for my future. For a short time I was blind, deaf, couldn't speak, and had to learn to breathe, talk, and walk again. My face was totally unrecognizable. But within six months, holding on to a promise from God, along with much love, care, and prayer, I was totally restored to health!

How wonderful to know that what seemed to be the end of my life was simply the beginning of a whole new journey, to be lived in intimate fellowship with God. A whole new and expanded destiny, to be fulfilled in Him.

Today and every new day ahead, may we with faithfulness, vulnerability, and transparency, allow God free access to our hearts—responding with trust, obedience, peace, love, and joy, that together we might continue to give Him greater access to speak to our hearts, that we like Abraham, might be known as "a friend of God."

When God Speaks to My Heart

A Daybook of
Personal Moments with God

My Precious One,

Ours is a close communion as between a father and his child, and you will find happiness in the freedom and ease of our relationship. Please do not forsake your time with Me, for I require devotion in such a friendship. It shall continue to bring us both overflowing joy. Rejoice, for this is the beginning of an even closer, intimate relationship with Me. My children who are called by My Name hear My voice. It is their inheritance. Come to Me with love and peace in your heart. Open unto Me the desires of your heart, your frustrations, your weaknesses, your blessings, and causes for rejoicing. Let Me share each and every response that you experience.

I Am Always With You,

Your Loving Father

Father,

Father, What areas of my life have I not readily shared with You?

I love You so much! Thank You for the promise of knowing You even more intimately. Help me, Father, to share with You my delight and excitement as You bless my life. Also, help me fully share with You my frustrations and weaknesses with transparency.

Amen

"My sheep hear My voice, and I know them, and they follow Me."
John 10:27 NKJV

Day 2

Dear One,

Cherish this time with Me. It will be like none other. I will speak to you in the day and I will speak to you in the night hours. Our time together shall be precious and well spent. Let Me direct your days, detail-by-detail. The enemy will try to get in, but he cannot. My power is greater, and you shall be aware of My Presence moment-by-moment, day-by-day. Cease your striving and come into peace with Me. You have come a long way, and the best is yet to come.

I Love You,

Your Father

Dear Father,

I see a picture of striving as a small child riding a tricycle. There is such a look of consternation and determination on her face, as she pedals with all of her might. Then, there is the picture of a small child being pushed by her Father and laughing with pure joy, with legs outstretched in freedom and absolute trust that her Daddy has everything under control! I like the second picture best! Truly, Father, the best is yet to come!

Loving Father, I do cherish this time with You, as You speak to my heart! Help me approach this time in absolute trust.

Amen

> *"You have made known to me the ways of life;*
> *You will enrapture me (diffusing my soul with joy)*
> *with and in Your presence."*
> Acts 2:28 AMP

When God Speaks to My Heart

My Dear One,

My guidance is yours for the asking. I delight in guiding My children. Simply walk step-by-step in expectation. The more revelation and awareness you walk in, the more you will receive. It is an ever increasing spiral upward of joy. The one who walks in expectation receives much. Therefore, walk expecting My guiding hand upon your life, moment-by-moment, for it is yours. Those who expect little, receive little. Ask much, and you will receive much.

I Am Your Source, Receive!

Your Loving Father

Loving Father,

Father, Here I am in Your wonderful, peaceful Presence, joyfully expecting and asking, listening intently for Your guidance in my life.

You have said Your ways are full of life and joy to those who follow after them. Father, I seek that very freedom, gladness, joy, and peace that Your guidance and revelation bring! My expectations and delight in You are high! You have never failed me! I love You, Father!

Amen

"When the Holy Spirit, who is truth, comes, he shall guide you into all truth,"
John 16:13 TLB

Day 4

My Child,

Your focus on Me is vital. When your focus on Me is sharp, all else falls into line. Listen quietly. Still your inner being. I can overcome the outside disturbances, so you can hear My voice above the clatter, but it is in the stillness that real fellowship with Me is found. Communion with Me is a two-way street. It must be pursued with diligence and regularity. Do not let the trials of this world intervene. My light shall shine through all the dark corners. New areas of your life shall come to light that have not been revealed before. Fill your days with My Presence!

Listen To My Heart,

Your Loving Father

Father,

The greatest desire of my heart is to be continually in Your Presence, in constant communion with You. Thank You that You long for that kind of communion with me, too. Help me, I pray, to continually walk with a pliable, humble, and repentant spirit, relinquishing all burdens to You, that I might hear Your voice clearly.

Precious Father, Today I will begin to share every thought with You, my most faithful and loving friend, with a constant listening ear, knowing You will share Your heart with me.

Amen

"Call to Me, and I will answer you,
and show you great and mighty things,
which you do not know."
Jeremiah 33:3 NKJV

When God Speaks to My Heart

My Child,

Depend on Me. Walk with assurance and with a carefree attitude. Refuse to be uptight. Rebuke fear and doubt every time they show themselves. Fly like a butterfly: relaxed, free, joyful, and exuberant. Pour that exuberance out onto others, with love. Place your life in My hands. Go forth with confidence, knowing that I am in command and My Spirit is within you, guiding you. Continue to prepare, storing up My Words in your heart. Much is ahead.

Hold My Hand,

Your Loving Father

Father God,

Father, Starting today, I will turn my thoughts toward You moment-by-moment by:

Just thinking of You makes me smile with joy and delight. When I allow pressures to crowd in or forget to begin the day thinking of You and listening for Your precious voice, thank You for continuing to make me more sensitive to Your gentle nudgings. In those moments, turn me back to the joy and awareness of Your Presence.

Amen

"For the LORD will be your confidence,
And will keep your foot from being caught."
Proverbs 3:26 NKJV

My Child,

Quiet your spirit before Me each day. I will lead you into what must be done. Nothing shall be left unattended. Rejoice as each day builds upon another, for in that building comes strength, fortitude, and a resilient spirit. Growth isn't always easy, but is helped along with a quieted, peaceful, unruffled spirit. Let Me quiet your spirit each day and prepare it for the events of the day to come. Discuss each day with Me at its close and we shall grow together. Now carry on with My peace within you.

Loving You,

Your Father

Father,

I love sharing what is happening in my life with my "heart friends." But You are the One I should enjoy the most, sharing in the events and details of my life. No one can care about the details of my life like You do. Teach me—Father, I pray, to faithfully "download" and discuss the events of my life with You at the close of each day.

Father, What are the things that You long for me to share with You about my day?

Amen

"Blessed is the man whose strength is in You,
Whose heart is set on pilgrimage."
Psalm 84:5 NKJV

Day 7

Precious One,

Presumption can enter in when one bypasses a one-to-one relationship with Me. That person knows of Me, knows about Me, knows I am a gracious God, but has not spent enough time with Me to know My will. My ways are higher than the ways of man. Again I say, "Does My Word not say, if one desires wisdom, just ask and I shall supply it?" You can know My perfect will in any situation through My Word and communion with Me. Stand on that Word in faith and believe.

Know Me And My Ways!

Your Loving Father

Father,

I seek Your wisdom. The greatest desire of my heart is to be one who hears Your heart every moment of every day, to be faithful and true in everything I say and do.

Dear Father, Today I ask You for wisdom in these areas of my life:

Amen

"If any of you lacks wisdom, let him ask of God, who gives to all liberally and without reproach, and it will be given to him."
James 1:5 NKJV

Day 8

My Precious One,

I want you to know that I love you! It is My gift to you. Open your heart to My love and receive with it with thanksgiving. My love and commitment to you is absolute and unconditional. It is constant. It is filled with grace. Starting today, seek to know Me more fully—to recognize the value and significance of My love. Seek My love with tenacity. Seek My love with strength of purpose. Seek My love with an undaunted faith. Receive and believe!

Receive My Gift Of Love!

Your Loving Father

Loving Father,

Everywhere I look, there You are! Your love surrounds me completely! You are always there to speak to my heart with so much love, causing my heart to sing about everything! Miracles abound everywhere I look! Thank You, Father, for helping me to more fully know the value of Your love. I want to think Your thoughts, to listen always with strength of purpose and with the faith to receive everything You speak to my heart. I do love You, Father!

Father, I am listening eagerly. How can I love You more fully today?

Amen

"…God is love, and he who abides in love abides in God, and God in him."
1 John 4:16 NKJV

Day 9

My Precious One,

The way of the Cross, and the way of My heart and of My love, say, "Here is My heart; it is open to you. I will honor you, care for you, speak well of you, pray for you, protect you, and encourage you." Strength of character determines whether you will cover with My love, or will judge and uncover. Seek love on your life journey and find truth.

Love As I Love,

Your Loving Father

Thank You, Father,

For teaching me to walk out each day with Your kind of love, and to always offer compassion and forgiveness, walking in strength of character. Help me to not build walls of protection but to be vulnerable and transparent, to walk in honor in all I say and do.

Father, When I am tempted to become negative about another, help me remember that they are one of Your treasures. Show me how to lift them up to You and speak blessing over them instead.

Amen

"Since you have purified your souls in obeying the truth through the Spirit in sincere love of the brethren, love one another fervently with a pure heart."
1 Peter 1:22 NKJV

My Precious Child,

Teach others to be still and know Me with an assurance of My love and care. Strengthen the hearts and hands around you. Be a lighthouse of hope and freedom in such a way as to say, "You can do what He has created you to do and be." My love will set them free. My love is security. I will fulfill the need and bless, providing every day. My matchless love is the only way.

Be My Love, My Child!

Your Loving Father

Oh yes, Father,

This is the cry of my heart for everyone I love! Help me to show them that they have a destiny in You! I want them to know that they can hear Your loving voice and be assured of Your love and care. I want them to know that You are their protection, their provision, and the best friend they will ever have. Help me to strengthen hearts and hands around me and cause them to know You, intimately and with joy!!!

Loving Father, Cause me to know You more intimately and experience Your heart of love in a deeper, more complete way!

Amen

*"You will prepare and strengthen and
direct their hearts."*
Psalm 10:17 AMP

My Child,

Listen to My footsteps as I walk beside you or in front of you; if beside you, we walk, talk, and fellowship. If ahead, follow closely, for we forge new paths. Hear My footsteps ahead of you now. Listen closely, follow closely. Be alert and listening for My every move. It is not hard. Listen, watch Me up ahead and follow. Speak My Words, sleep My Words, follow My Words, and be My Words. The time is now to be what I have called you to be. I have called you to be a lighthouse of rest, by My Spirit of praise, which brings peace. Life and light spring forth from My Spirit of peace. Be a peace giver, and together we shall see lives changed, mountains moved, and My Kingdom proclaimed.

Follow Me, My Precious One!

Your Loving Father

Loving Father,

Help me to understand what it really means to walk victoriously with You! To realize the significance of speaking Your Words, sleeping Your Words, following Your Words, being Your Words, and being a peace giver.

Father, I do treasure Your written Word and Your spoken Word as You daily speak to my heart!

Amen

"But he who keeps (treasures) His Word, (who bears in mind His precepts, who observes His message in its entirety), truly in Him has the love of and for God been perfected (completed, reached maturity)."
1 John 2:5 AMP

Day 12

My Child,

My heart croons over you like a song of love, the melody sweet, with the fragrance of Heaven. Can you not hear it within, eliminating all stress and fear? Listen with your spirit. Open your heart to rejoice in the love I have for you. My heart yearns after you that you would know Me more intimately. Bask in the warmth of My love, positioned in the assurance of My promises. My love is a shield to you. My hand is upon you to bless you. The beauty of My love is real, and in Me there is a place of quiet, safe rest.

Your Loving Father

Father,

Help me to trust in Your love for me. Bring a new understanding of Your love into my life and strength to walk in confidence, even when my heart feels uncertain.

Amen

Today, I will lay all my cares aside and turn my thoughts toward God by:

"...I have loved you with an everlasting love."
Jeremiah 31:3 NKJV

When God Speaks to My Heart

My Devoted Child,

You have sailed many a weary hour. Release unto Me all your fears for the future and race alongside Me with a boundless trust and freedom. Hold fast to My hand and face the wind with a heart full of renewed courage. You are not alone. My strength is yours, and it will carry you through unscathed. The race goes well for the strong of heart. Press forward. The way is clear ahead. You shall arrive on time. Set sail with a new determination to finish the trip to the end. It is there you will find victory.

Forever By Your Side,

Your Loving Father

Father,

I give these areas of concern to You this day, Lord:

I hand over my concerns to You. Help me to look to You, instead of to my burdens, when I am tempted to worry. Teach me to trust in You completely, and to rest in Your guiding hand. I love You.

Amen

"…Those who wait on the LORD, Shall renew their strength; They shall mount up with wings like eagles, They shall run and not be weary, They shall walk and not faint."
Isaiah 40:31 NKJV

Day 14

My Child,

Listen to the rustling of the trees when the breezes blow. It is the trees sighing against the pressure of the wind. They bend but they do not break. When the breezes stop blowing, once again they stand tall and powerful, knowing when the wind blows once again they are prepared for the onslaught because they are flexible. They don't take the pressure of the wind personally. They don't feel that the wind is out to defeat them. Stand watch on your heart to remain in a state of forgiveness. Seek not acceptance for yourself, but give acceptance, and reach out in love and compassion.

With Love,

Your Father

Loving Father,

Help me to avoid looking to others for the acceptance and approval that only You can give. Show me how to faithfully reach out to others with forgiveness, acceptance, love, and compassion. Though the storms of life will come, cause me to be stronger and more loving, always trusting You.

Father, When I feel my heart becoming anxious, I will come to You with the trust of a child and say:

Amen

"Great peace have those who love Your law,
And nothing causes them to stumble."
Psalm 119:165 NKJV

Day 15

My Child,

Lighten your load even further as you come into My Presence daily. Start out with a clean slate each day by giving everything back to Me. Let Me take each day and make of it a picture and creation of My love. Sights and sounds, blessings abound, each and every day. At the end of every day, I will smile at you, My child, and say, "You did it My way! You are blessed!!!"

I Love You,

Your Father

Father,

Father, What other ways can I totally relinquish each day to You?

At the beginning of every day, help me give back to You all of my responsibilities, cares, unfinished business, have to's, want to's, longings, indecisions—everything—that You might moment by moment lead me into what You want me to be and accomplish that day.

Amen

"You will show me the path of life;
In Your presence is fullness of joy;
At Your right hand are pleasures forevermore."
Psalm 16:11 NKJV

Day 16

My Child,

Be still and know that I am God. The child who trusts and obeys his parents enjoys many more privileges. So it is in the Kingdom of God. The child who takes in My Word and obeys it, walks in much more from Me than the child who lets things come and go as they may. I am the rewarder of those who diligently seek Me. Continue digesting My Word. Walk with the assurance, My child, that I am with you this day. My love will surround you as you go about your day. Enter into My blessings. Walk fully in them. Listen for My voice.

I Love You, My Child,

Your Father

Loving Father,

I love the way You teach me, in reading Your Word cover to cover, version after version. Every day, a feast, as I've delighted in the treasures from Your heart to mine through Your Scriptures, Your Word! Reading Your Word and hearing Your voice—nothing compares!

Father, You always have a strategy. How would You have me study, absorb, and enjoy Your Word now?

Amen

"...I am your Shield, your abundant compensation, and your reward shall be exceedingly great."
Genesis 15:1 AMP

My Faithful Child,

Blessed is the one whose heart seeks after Me in anticipation and desire to know Me better. His spirit shall be like a well-watered plant thriving in the sunshine. You are blessed, My child. Let your blessings flow out to those around you. Many shall the blessings be and many shall bless My Name because of your faithfulness. Reach out and minister in a spirit of love and forgiveness. Press on into My Kingdom, giving forth My blessings.

I Love You,

Your Father

Father,

Loving Father, My heart is listening with anticipation and joy!

I so hunger to know You more. I pray for more confidence, to allow Your blessings to flow over to those around me. Show me tangible ways to touch the lives of others, and how to pray for them, knowing that You will answer with Your heart of love! Help me pray for others as easily as I breathe!

Amen

"As the hart pants and longs for the water brooks,
so I pant and long for You, O God."
Psalm 42:1 AMP

Day 18

My Beloved Child,

Search the Scriptures and know the intricacies of My Word. Let Me point out to you the nuances that will fulfill the desires of your heart and cause you to grow. My Word is truly an open door to you that cannot be closed. Let go of the trials in life, and grasp tightly to My Word. Yes, a new day has begun, and the burden you have known shall fade away into the distance, as the vista of the new day opens before you.

You Are Blessed Beyond Measure,

Your Father

Father,

Help me to make my heart a storehouse for Your Word. Point out to me the nuances and wonderful intricacies of Your Word, to delight and fulfill my heart desires and cause me to grow even more. You are ever faithful, my loving Father!

Loving Father, What do You want to share with me today? I am listening with delight!

Amen

"If you abide in Me, and My words abide in you, you will ask what you desire, and it shall be done for you."
John 15:7 NKJV

My Precious Child,

Will to know My Word. It is an open door for you that will never close. My Word is nourishment, it is strength, it builds faith, and it is the source through which questions are answered. It is the source of all wisdom and knowledge. Grow in it. My Word is the instrument through which you shall grow steady. My Word is the source of life, eternal and abundant. Know that I am your God. I love you. You need not ever be afraid. I am always with you, guiding in every thought, word, and action. The things of this world will fade away, but My Word abides forever. Walk fully in it.

I Am With You Always,

Your Loving Father

Dear Father,

As I read Your Word, help me to know You as a faithful and loving Father, whom I can trust with all my heart. As I read and sing Your Word, help me to hear Your guiding Word in my heart. Thank You, Father, for being such a loving God!

Father, I desire to follow You. Guide me today…ever closer to you.

Amen

"Your Word is a lamp to my feet
and a light to my path."
Psalm 119:105 AMP

My Child,

My love and My Word are inseparable. One cannot fully be manifested without the other. Love, given without My Word, is incomplete. My Word, without My love, is deficient. It is the union of both My love and My Word that brings forth abundance, fulfillment, peace, and My perfect joy. Be a restorer of My love, brought forth through My Word. Enjoy the life I have for you to its fullness.

Be My Word And My Love,

Your Loving Father

Loving Father,

As I continue my adventure with You, I seek to place Your Word upon my heart. I want to grow in faith. Faith in Your Word leads to the greatest action of all, loving with Your love, which brings life! Thank You, Father, for the gifts of Your Word.

Father, Thank You for opening new realms of Your Word and Your love to me today. My heart is open to receive.

Amen

"Your word have I laid up in my heart,
that I might not sin against You."
Psalm 119:11 AMP

Day 21

My Child,

Seek Me daily in My Word and in My promises—let them be your pillar of strength. My strength is your strength, and in My Word is that strength. Stand on it, My child, unwavering, and strength shall be yours. Let My Word saturate your being. Let it be the sustenance that energizes and moves you. My Word—your life and very being! Rejoice in the Word that is in your heart. It is there to sustain you and to cause you to grow in strength each day. Go forth in the strength of My Word!

I Love You,

Your Father

Precious Father,

Father, Help me receive Your strength through Your Word today.

Your Word truly is my life and very being! It brings me strength when there seems to be no energy left in me. Your promises bring me hope. But, most of all, having intimate communion with You is life! Thank You for always being there for me! I love You, Father!

Amen

"The Lord is my Strength and song; and He has become my Salvation."
Psalm 118:14 AMP

Day 22

Dear One,

Can you hear My voice? Are you walking in My way? My way shines as a beacon of light. Are you tottering on the borderline? Follow Me and hear My Words of love. Lean on Me and My Word, and keep your heart full to overflowing. Let your life become a beacon of light drawing others to Me.

I Love You,

Your Father

Loving Father,

It is so exciting to hear Your loving voice of encouragement and wisdom, love and hope! Help me to share that same encouragement with those around me. You are so wonderful, Father!

Beloved Father, Teach my ears to hear even more clearly, I pray, as You speak to my heart!

Amen

"...and they will listen to My voice and heed My call...."
John 10:16 AMP

My Child,

Be a communicator of My Words through thought, word, and deed. Stand tall in My Spirit flanked on either side by the strength of My love. Speak My Words of life to others around you. Be a processor and distributor of My Word! Present them with My Words, which bring transformation…beautiful illustrations and pictures that can both be seen and understood. Beauty for ashes, a heart filled with hope for a new day—that has been My gift to you. Release it to others.

Be My Love,

Your Loving Father

Loving Father,

Father, Who would You have me speak to this day? Who can I reach out to, reflecting who You are in everything I say and do?

You have always said that the purity of heart (thoughts) and actions (deeds) always speak louder than words! But, Father, thank You for also anointing my words, to deliver beautiful portraits of Your wonderful love and care to others! Thank You for helping me to stand confidently in Your Spirit, and to speak Your Words of life, hope, and restoration.

Amen

"A man has joy in making an apt answer, and a word spoken at the right moment—how good it is!"
Proverbs 15:23 AMP

Day 24

My Child,

Radiate My peace! Seek My peace. Search for its richness and fulfillment. Make My peace readily available, easily seen upon your countenance and displayed in your life. My peace will become the visible entity in your life that others will hunger for. Liberally share it and My Name—that others will be blessed, warmed, and softened by it and thus receive My love. Light the fire of understanding in many, through your constant pursuit and demonstration of My peace.

With Love,

Your Father

Father,

Thank You for teaching me to walk in peace, day-by-day and moment-by-moment. Thank You for forgiving me when I become anxious. Help me to remember to come back to Your embrace, to return to that place of peace, calm, and trust that comes from You.

Faithful Father, Show me Your supernatural peace today.

Amen

You will keep him in perfect peace
Whose mind is stayed on You,
Because he trusts in You.
Isaiah 26:3 NKJV

When God Speaks to My Heart

Day 25

My Child,

It is My passion for you to experience a fulfilled life of love, truth, and faith. There is a fine line between faith and presumption. Faith calls forth those things that have been proclaimed by the Spirit of God. Presumption calls forth that which has been made known by the notion of man. Be the friend of faith and the foe of presumption. Your heart will know the difference. Listen to your heart and respond appropriately. I will always make truth known through love. If you see love is lacking, so is truth. First comes love, then comes truth. Reversed, truth is not revealed, but a heart that *needs* love. Sincere love and absolute truth go hand in hand.

Walk In My Love!

Your Loving Father

Loving Father,

Your Words of wisdom bring such joy and understanding to my heart! And so it has been, dear Father, that as I seek You for answers, You present them to me with clarity and understanding that I might continue to learn Your ways of truth and faith, through Your love!

Loving Father, Show me how to live my life out in faith, truth, and love, as You speak to my heart!

Amen

"…and though I have all faith, so that I could remove mountains, but have not love, I am nothing."
1 Corinthians 13:2 NKJV

Day 26

My Child,

Master the art of maintaining open-ended plans, that My plans might always become and remain paramount in your life. My plans for you are as vast as the expanse of the ocean and unrestricted. Let loose of your plans and let Me take hold of the helm. Follow with dexterity and delight—your hand in Mine. Let Me lead in all things. Let Me bring forth your future creatively and freely.

Fly Free, My Child!

Your Loving Father

Loving Father,

What a wonderful way to live, following You with dexterity and delight, no longer being bound by closed-ended plans that often stagnate and cease to function. I am free to sail into the wind, letting You take hold of the helm! Let the adventure begin! I love You, Father!

Father, My life is in Your loving, protective hands! Thank You, Father, for speaking to my heart, as we walk that plan out together!

Amen

"He led them forth by the straight and right way."
Psalm 107:7 AMP

When God Speaks to My Heart

Day 27

My Precious Child,

Walk your life out as a shining banner held high. Set a standard for life! Set a standard for love — unconditional! Set a standard for peace — a peace unruffled by circumstances. Set a standard for joy — My radiance brought forth by My Presence! Set a standard for wisdom — brought forth by the guidance of My Spirit. Walk your life out in confidence through communion with Me!

I Am With You Always,

Your Loving Father

Loving Father,

I want to walk my life out with integrity. I want to be a shining standard. Help me fasten my gaze on You. Show me how to walk out my life each and every day — upright and pleasing to You, in a gentle, contagious way.

Beloved Father, Show me examples in my life where I can be an example of Your standard:

Amen

"He who walks uprightly walks securely,"
Proverbs 10:9 AMP

Day 28

My Precious One,

Do you know you are sealed in My love? It is a place of security and safety. Learn to listen to Me and hear My heart of love with a new intensity—with every fiber of your being fixed on Me. Secure within your heart, the knowledge of My love. It cannot be diminished. It is! Let it emanate from within you, unlimited by what was, what is, or what will be. My love is! Continue to rest in My love and grow in the grace and peace of My love. It will hold you steady and secure. Relax in My embrace. You will be amazed at what I am doing in and through your life. Enjoy the ride!

You Are My Delight!

Your Loving Father

Loving Father,

I seek to listen to Your heart and to grasp the encompassing and unconditional love You have for me. Help me to fully receive and understand how much You treasure me—that You delight in me. I want to become strong and confident in Your love for me. Even in the midst of trials and struggles, sustain my heart with a knowing and joy that I am Your beloved child!

Faithful Father, There is so much on my heart to share with You:

Amen

[He has also appropriated and acknowledged us as His by] putting His seal upon us and giving us His [Holy] Spirit in our hearts as the security deposit and guarantee [of the fulfillment of His promise].
2 Corinthians 1:22 AMP

My Precious Child,

Stand strong in My peace and keep the light of praise burning. Enter into My peace through the avenue of praise—a sure way into My Presence. Go forth strong in the foundation of My truth and My love. My peace is your strength. It comes down upon you as a magnificent blanket of purity, to wash away the contaminants of the world.

Be At Peace, My Precious Child,

Your Loving Father

Beloved Father,

Father, Thank You that I can enjoy Your peace 24 hours a day!

You are the love of my life! I praise You with honor and devotion, and thank You for Your all-encompassing, wonderful peace, which is my strength. Thank You that Your peace is a magnificent blanket of purity, to wash away the contaminants of my life. But most of all, Father, thank You for Your precious Presence. I love You, Father!

Amen

*"and the peace of God, which surpasses
all understanding, will guard your hearts
and minds through Christ Jesus."*
Philippians 4:7 NKJV

My Precious Child,

The more you praise, the more you love. The more you love, the more you praise. They reproduce each other. Allow praise to flow from your lips as streams of living water, watering the dry land. Those walking in the desert shall be drawn to Me through your praise, and through the love that praise produces. Praise Me! Praise Me!

You Are My Treasure,

Your Loving Father

Loving Father,

I praise You, love, honor, bless, and thank You, for Your life poured out on me and through me to others! I long to be Your messenger of love. I will praise You, O Lord, with my whole heart forever!

I love You, Father, and my desire is to love as You love.

Amen

*"I will praise, You, O Lord, with my whole heart;
I will show forth (recount and tell aloud) all
Your marvelous works and wonderful deeds!"*
Psalm 9:1 AMP

Day 31

Dear Child,

It is going to be fun—an adventure! See Me place the desire in your heart, and be encouraged as you see it come to pass. Stand encouraged. Now is the time to rejoice and go forward in joy. It is truly a new day with new ways. Release unto Me your cares, for I have given you a spirit of delight. Be refreshed, My beloved one, and continue on in this journey of life, with renewed vision and vigor. I love you!

You Are Precious To Me,

Your Loving Father

Precious Father,

I love You, Father! Thank You for speaking to my heart!

You bring such delight and joy to my life. Take residence in my heart. And thank You, Father, for renewed vision and energy. My heart longs to know You more!

Amen

"May Christ through your faith [actually] dwell
(settle down, abide, make His permanent home)
in your hearts! May you be rooted deep
in love and founded securely on love."
Ephesians 3:17 AMP

My Child,

Stand steady and firm, and do not give up your steady stance of strength—strength upon the strong foundation of My Word. Whisk confusion out the window. Steady strength and assurance are your portion. I will deal with inconsistencies. You be consistent in Me. I will calm the storm and still the turbulent seas, and bring justification and vindication. Fear not, but continue steady, day by day.

I Am With You!

Your Father

Thank You, Father,

You keep me steady and secure when everything around me seems unsteady and insecure. Your love secures me and shelters me when the storms blow. Thank You for teaching me patience and trust in the midst of the storm. And, Father, thank You for Your Word that empowers my life!

Dear Father, I give these concerns to You:

Amen

"You will not need to fight in this battle. Position yourselves, stand still and see the salvation of the LORD, who is with you."
2 Chronicles 20:17 NKJV

My Child,

Fill your life with My music, joy, and song, and splash it onto others with freedom and liberality. A life filled with joy and song has no room for criticism and negativism. Laughter pushes out darkness. Join into My joy, freedom, and abundance, and know that all is within My timetable and care. Be still and know that I am God, and I am the rewarder of those who diligently seek Me. Stand fast upon My Word and rejoice in the fulfillment of that Word.

You Are Blessed!

Your Loving Father

Father,

Loving Father, You have blessed me so much! How can I bless You today?

You have done such great things for me, day after day, year after year. When I find myself feeling weak and tired, all I have to do is laugh, and strength amazingly pours in. Laughter is such a gift from You. Thank You, Lord, for giving me friends who love to laugh with me, another priceless gift that only You can give.

Amen

"Then were our mouths filled with laughter, and our tongues with singing. Then they said among the nations, The Lord has done great things for them. The Lord has done great things for us! We are glad!"
Psalm 126:2-3 AMP

My Blessed Child,

A songbird chirps and sings, welcoming each new day with song. He announces each new morning with joy and exuberance. So are you to sing with joy, proclaiming My loving works to a sleepy world. Continue to sing, announcing the blessings of each new day. Just as birds are unafraid and confident in their freedom, they sing and fly high undaunted by the tactics of their predators. You too can sound forth My love and faithfulness. You can joyfully share My ability to heal and restore. Go forth in My Name, proclaiming from the most sincere place of your heart, that there is a place of quiet rest, safe in the arms of God!

Be Confident In My Love!

Your Loving Father

Loving Father,

Help me to start each new day with praise and thanksgiving in my heart…to call forth each new day with joy, exuberance, and faith. Help me, just like the songbirds, to be unafraid and confident in my newfound freedom, knowing there is a place of safety and quiet rest in Your arms of love. I love You, Father!

I will praise You, Father, with my whole heart and tell of all Your blessings in my life.

Amen

"I will praise You, O Lord, with my whole heart;
I will show forth (recount and tell aloud)
all Your marvelous works and wonderful deeds!"
Psalm 9:1 AMP

My Blessed Child,

Sunshine and flowers, beauty and grace; it's going to be a wonderful place! As you seek My face every day, I will show you a new way, and you will navigate the way with great delight. What seems out of sight now, will become clear and rise up to meet you. So be joyful, My child. It is all under My control. I've been making you complete and whole to rise to every occasion with strength of character, peace, wisdom, and love. Strength of character, yes; strength of purpose, yes; and the strength of My love permeating your being. Stand fast and full of courage wherever you go.

I Take Pleasure In You, My Child,

Your Loving Father

Father,

Loving Father, My heart sings to You a song of love with thankfulness and praise!

You have said, "Stand still, and know that I am God." And so, Father, it has been to the joy and delight of my heart to trust in You. Even when the way is dark, You are there, lighting my way. I love You, Father!

Amen

"I am the Lord your God, Who has brought you out of the land of Egypt, out of the house of bondage."
Exodus 20:2 AMP

My Precious One,

Relax in My Presence, and lift up your heart to Me with steadfast love and adoration. Let Me be your place of habitation, just as you are Mine. I am your steadfast rock of protection. There is a cleft in that rock for you. Nestle into that cleft with trust and love, as a child snuggles into his parent's lap for warmth and affirmation. I long to be that quiet place of rest and affirmation for you. Rest in Me, child. Rest in Me. When you have rested and learned of that quietness in Me, then we can proudly step out together in service and in love. Learn of My love for you, child. Rely on and receive deeper levels of that love. It is yours. Receive, and then become a restorer, an instrument of restoring that love to the brethren. It is yours, My child. Reach out and receive it.

You Are Precious To Me,

Your Loving Father

Loving Father,

There is no place I would rather be than quietly snuggled next to Your heart, listening to Your heartbeat, trusting You with the trust of a child, and listening to Your loving Words of affirmation to my heart. Thank You, Father, for drawing me daily to that treasured place. Thank You for teaching me daily deeper levels of Your all-encompassing love.

Precious Father, My heart reaches out to You with love and adoration, thanksgiving and joy!

Amen

Jehovah is my rock, and my fortress, and my deliverer;
My God, my rock, in whom I will take refuge;
My shield, and the horn of my salvation, my high tower.
Psalm 18:2 ASV

My Child,

Look out at the panorama before you. Soak in its exquisiteness. See the ups and the downs, the hills, mountains, and valleys, and the areas clouded by haze. It is all beautiful. So is your life. Every day, every hour, every minute, every second, is a divine product of My perfect plan for your life. Some meanings are hidden by the soft haze, but they, too, are important and significant in My sight. The ups and downs, the hills, mountains, and valleys, form the splendor that is so pleasing to the eye. So it is with you. I am forming beauty in your life, beauty that will last and be a blessing forever. Relish and enjoy the formation. I am imprinting My beauty upon your life—body, soul, and spirit. Enjoy the process through faith, love, peace, joy, and trust. My very best is yours to enjoy. Continue on, My child, with My grace sustaining and leading you to victory.

I Am With You!

Your Loving Father

My Father,

Father, Today I will focus on seeing Your beauty in each and every occurrence of the day, listening closely to Your voice speaking to my heart:

As I look out over the panorama before me, help me to see my life as You do—all coming together to make a beautiful portrait of Your divine purpose for me. Each night as I talk over the events of the day with You, I am in awe at the intricacy of each detail of my life, and my heart reaches out to You with gratefulness and love. Thank You, Father, for Your loving care!

Amen

"He has made everything beautiful in its time."
Also He has put eternity in their hearts,"
Ecclesiastes 3:11 NKJV

A Daybook of Personal Moments With God

Day 38

My Child,

Let love be your aim in all things. Release your burdens, rejections, disappointments, and disunities unto Me. Let Me carry them. Don't hold any of them to yourself. Drop them into My arms in an eternity of forgetfulness. Live only in the joy of this moment with Me, with My love; for what is past is past, totally past. You have a loving, peaceful, and pure present, if you allow it to be. Love all others sincerely. Sincerity comes from a pure, undefiled heart, from which all contaminants have been released unto Me. So go forth this day, resting in the assurance of My love, freely bestowing that same love upon others, unrestricted by the past or your cares for the future.

Love With My Love, My Child,

Your Father

Loving Father,

What a wonderful way to live, releasing every burden, rejection, disappointment, and disunity unto You, and letting You carry them! That makes it possible to see and love everyone with purity of heart, with no history of hurts or disappointments, simply loving each one as You love them, unrestricted by the past or the future, which leaves simply the loving, peaceful, and pure present. What a wonderful, loving, exciting life You give us to live, Precious Father!

Father, I give You every rejection that I have held on to, even unknowingly, and put them in a basket like dead leaves, and give the basket to You!

Amen

"Let your love be sincere (a real thing)."
Romans 12:9 AMP

When God Speaks to My Heart

My Child,

I am bringing balance to your life—balance for the journey. Balance to know that your expectations rest in Me and not in others. Balance to know that your peace rests in Me and My ability to come through. Balance without need to fear or worry. Balance to know that in your joy is strength. Balance to always enjoy the ride without expectations. Balance to be able to laugh in all circumstances. Balance to walk in trust and faithfulness at all times. Balance to remain safe and secure in My arms of love. Worry and doubt will always be far removed from you, as you, each day, take the stand to trust, believe, and freely receive My Spirit of love as a part of everything you think, do, and say.

I Love You,

Your Father

Loving Father,

Thank You for bringing balance to my life. I will trust You completely for every detail in the journey of my life. I love You!

Father, When I find myself once again unsettled, I will turn to You with trust.

Amen

"Let me be weighed in a just balance,
That God may know my integrity...."
Job 31:6 NKJV

My Child,

Let go of the past! Walk into the future with great joy and freedom. My strength is with you for a preordained future. Strain not to see too far in the distance. Walk in peace with Me, fulfilling My call upon your life in small ways each day that build upon themselves to create all that I have predestined for you. Little bits each day establish the finished creation. The door shall open on time and you will go through at the appointed time. Confer with Me often in the times to come, for My wisdom shall come forth to confirm and establish you in all that you should do and pursue.

I Go Before You,

Your Loving Father

Loving Father,

I seek Your peace and strength of character, that I might be content to let You add each significant piece day after day, to produce the finished creation of my life and destiny. It gives me such peace and joy to know that You have preordained my life and that You will establish me in all that I should do and pursue. I love You!

Father, What is on Your heart for me to know today?

Amen

"For the vision is yet for an appointed time and it hastens to the end [fulfillment]; it will not deceive or disappoint. Though it tarry, wait [earnestly] for it, because it will surely come;"
Habakkuk 2:3 AMP

My Child,

Walk with Me. Extend your faith and trust Me with all of your heart. Avoid letting your mind seek to box Me in, or to try and figure out each detail. Far better be it to walk with a constant awareness of My Presence and My guidance than to strive and worry over the future. With faith you can walk with assurance, without fear or apprehension. So are you to walk.

I Am Guiding You, My Child,

Your Loving Father

Loving Father,

Father, I am coming into Your Presence once again today, quieting my heart, loving You!

You have said, "Lean not unto your own understanding, but reach out for My understanding and wisdom. Resort not to blind decisions. Reach out to Me for My direction in all things. Be sensitive to the nudgings of My Spirit. Run not in circles." Thank You, that when I walk in constant awareness of Your Presence and Your guidance, I can walk without fear or apprehension. I can walk with faith that You are always with me, helping me to make the right decisions. When I find myself running in circles, I will slow down and once again come into Your Presence, with peace.

Amen

"Now faith is the substance of things hoped for,
the evidence of things not seen."
Hebrews 11:1 NKJV

Dear Child,

Be faithful to start each day right by bringing it to Me, and to end each day right, by discussing it with Me. This will amplify the sweetness of each day and give you a greater understanding of the day from My perspective. Trials will be averted and your life mission amplified. Stick with it, My child. The rewards far exceed the struggle, and I will be with you every step of the way! My delights shall fill your heart with joy, and My Presence shall continue to fill your heart with love.

I Love You!

Your Father

Father,

You are so precious to my heart. You are always so encouraging and loving. Thank You, Father, for the peace and the joy rising up in my soul with a new sense of strength, life, beauty, and contentment. Thank You, Lord, I am so grateful!

Dear, dear Father, I lift this day up to You.

Amen

"Surely the righteous shall give thanks to Your name;
The upright shall dwell in Your presence."
Psalm 140:13 NKJV

My Child,

Spend time with Me. Enjoy My Presence. My pleasure is in you. Get to know Me and learn of My gentleness, passion, beauty, faithfulness, and grace. Grow with My love. Remain steadfast. Continue step by step in the way you are going, no matter what the circumstances—and I will be there with you.

I Love You Too, Child!

Your Father

Father,

Father, When the struggles of life try to overcome me with their loud demands, I will remember to stay in Your Presence, steadfast and secure, by:

I love You, too! Nothing is more pleasurable in life than having these times with You, Father! Truly in Your Presence is fullness of joy. My heart sings with the pleasure Your Presence brings. Thank You for this peaceful habitation in Your heart.

Amen

"You will make me full of joy in Your presence."
Acts 2:28 NKJV

Day 44

My Child,

Stay awhile, My child. Let Me enjoy the warmth of your smile. New trails aren't easy, I know, but I am with you wherever you go, directing your path—I have a plan, the outcome secure. There is nothing to fear. Continue to stand in without a care to know you are safe wherever you go. Be at peace and you will continue to hear My Words of love upon your ear. Sing My Words of love in your heart, to keep your spirits high in all you do. Songs of love sustain the soul, that you may remain secure and whole.

My Love Surrounds You,

Your Loving Father

Father,

You give such loving confidence! You have fashioned me to draw close to Your heart with peace and undistracted love, with the trust of a child. When I come near to Your heart, my whole body, soul, and spirit exprience peace and rest. I know that all will be well, as I take it step by step without fear or apprehension. You give peace, not as the world gives peace, but as a loving Father gives peace to His treasured, adored child.

Father, When I feel anxious, I will find that place of loving peace and rest close to Your heart.

Amen

"Serve the LORD with gladness;
Come before His Presence with singing."
Psalm 100:2 NKJV

When God Speaks to My Heart

Day 45

My Child,

Faith that is firm is also patient! Let patience have its way in your life. Let faith stand tall in your heart, statuesque and immovable. Stand firm, stand fast, stand tall, with the assurance that My will shall come to pass in My time, not thine. Frantic hurriedness brings mistakes and failure. Patiently pressing on brings My victory and My success. Be that patient, consistent child, for together we shall win!

I Love You, My Child,

Your Heavenly Father

Father,

Loving Father, I have quieted my spirit within me to listen patiently to Your heart.

Your Word gives me such peace of heart. Help me to remove impatience, uncertainty, and doubt from my life. You have led me in the past and I know You will continue. Help me be on my guard against frenzied activity. Your way is a quiet assurance. Show me how to confidently walk one step at a time, steadfastly and firmly, with love and compassion.

Amen

"But let endurance and steadfastness and patience
have full play and do a thorough work, so that you
may be [people] perfectly and fully developed
[with no defects], lacking in nothing."
James 1:4 AMP

Dear Child,

Joy is your portion. I have proclaimed it to be so. My joy is ever there for you to pick up and relish with abandonment and freedom. It is ever My gift to you, always there to put on and relish. Joy walks hand in hand with peace. Peace and joy, the signature of the knowledge of My love.

You Are Loved!

Your Father

Loving Father,

You have said that our lives are to be "portraits" of Your love. My desire is to consistently walk in Your joy and peace no matter what is going on in my life, trusting You with the outcome in every instance. Thank You for helping me to choose to walk in joy, with abandonment and freedom. I am Your joyful child!

How can I bring more joy to You, Father?

Amen

"These things I have spoken to you, that My joy may remain in you, and that your joy may be full."
John 15:11 NKJV

My Child,

Do you know the purpose of waiting and patience? Learn to trust in My love and goodness for you, and know that I will never forsake you or allow you to miss My best for you. My timing is everything, and what I have promised will come forth in perfect timing. I will give you My best, not second best. I will fulfill what I have promised. Believe this! Patience gives way to strength, and strength makes a way for truth. I am changing you from the inside out. The cares of this world will become less and less important. You are learning that it is not what *you* do, but what *I* do for and with you that matters.

I Love You, My Child,

Your Father

Father,

Father, Thank You for helping me to always bring my impatience to You, knowing Your timing is perfect.

It's an adventure of a lifetime walking moment by moment with You. Thank You that every detail of my life is important to You. Teach me that time is my friend, and will continue to be until the end—that I don't need to worry about the how, when, or where, because You will continue to lead and guide me every step of the way. Every day is a treasure to behold.

Amen

"But let patience have its perfect work, that you may be perfect and complete, lacking nothing."
James 1:4 NKJV

Dear Child,

Today is a time for reflection and a total acceptance of My love for you. A total acceptance of My love in all that you do. Spend time with Me, hear My voice and get to know Me more each day. It's called intimacy. Without it there is no relationship. An open heart invites intimacy and causes the walls to come down in your heart. An open heart is a loving heart. An open heart has no fear. Be My open heart to My people, and they will recognize the pain and fear they have let come in, causing them to build walls, which also keeps love out. Show them to Me by loving them, and they'll begin to realize what My love is all about. They will begin to feel and see what it really means to be secure and free.

Love them to Me!

Your Loving Father

Father,

Every day You bring such joy to my heart and an excitement in the understanding of how we are to live. There is nothing on earth that I enjoy and love more than intimate conversations with You. Thank You for putting such a love in my heart for Your treasures, Your people. Thank You for teaching me to love them as You do.

Father, How would You have me more effectively open my heart to those You bring to me?

Amen

*"Then I will give them a heart to know Me,
that I am the LORD; and they shall be
My people, and I will be their God...."
Jeremiah 24:7 NKJV*

Day 49

My Child,

Continue listening with your whole heart—wide open and unafraid of repercussions, just loving for love's sake. Yes, My child, it's the only way to live. It's the only way to give, loving with no expectations. With that kind of love, no rejection, bitterness, anger, hurt, or judgment can grow. That kind of love is free and pure, filled with joy and contentment in the giving. Nothing negative can stick to that kind of love. It brings honor, healing, and joy wherever it goes. Freedom rings and sings in a heart that is pure and loving, as I love.

Love As I Love!

Your Loving Father

Father,

Father, What else would You have me know about love?

It is so hard to love without expectations, but so worth it to have no residue of bitterness, anger, hurt, judgment, or rejection. Whenever I am tempted to feel any of these things, I will look to You and remember I am loving, in partnership with the Creator of the Universe, Who loves me unconditionally. Thank You for loving me so much!

Amen

"Love never fails."
1 Corinthians 13:8 NKJV

My Child,

I have placed in your heart a seed that thrives and grows—the seed of love. There can be no love without honor; honor for Me, for yourself, and for others. Love without honor is manipulation, control, lust, or fear. Without honor, expectations are often met with disappointment. Let only words of love, honor, blessing, appreciation, and truth come from your mouth. Words that uplift and bring hope. Words that bring blessing and not a curse. Words that reverse the curse. Words that bring healing to the heart, body, and soul. Words that complete and make whole. Words that make the heart sing. My child, be not only a word picture of My love to the world, but also an example of honor that transforms the world.

Speak Words Of Honor And Love,

Your Loving Father

Dear Father,

I pray that only positive, uplifting words of blessing come from my heart and mouth. Words that bring healing, that complete and make whole. Words that edify and make the heart sing; words of honor, appreciation, and truth. That I would speak only as You would speak, whether it be with meekness or boldness, that they would be only words from Your heart. I love You!

Father, When I am tempted to say words that are not from Your heart, please stop me in Your own precious way, that I will recognize:

Amen

"By this all will know that you are My disciples, if you have love for one another."
John 13:35 NKJV

Day 51

Dear One,

It is called honor! Honor My wishes! Honor those around you and honor yourself! Seek to walk in honor in all that you do and say. Dishonor destroys. Honor, however, brings life and wholeness. Discernment is recognizing dishonor. Trials come from dishonor. No longer will dishonor sneak up on you or entrap you. You shall recognize it for what it is—lack of love. Walk with honor.

You Are Loved,

Your Father

Father,

Thank You, Father, for wisdom and discernment as I come to You each day.

Thank You for giving me added discernment for the journey of life. My desire is to honor others as You have honored me. You love me, not because I deserve Your love, but simply because You love me. Thank You for teaching me to recognize dishonor in all its forms.

Amen

"The fear of the LORD is the instruction of wisdom,
And before honor is humility."
Proverbs 15:33 NKJV

Day 52

My Child,

Express your needs and your views more clearly and precisely to Me. In this way we can more fully work together, building trust and faith as we go. Do not be afraid of your negative feelings, for as you express and share them with Me, I can respond with the answer you need. Negatives held within remain negative and increase in their damaging power. Negatives brought to the surface and expressed to Me can then be transformed into positives in your life. Do not hide your feelings from Me. Express them that they might be dealt with to your growth and to My glory.

Share Your Heart With Me,

Your Loving Father

Father,

The desire of my heart is to stretch out my arms to You in total submission, speaking freely what is on my heart—my doubts, needs, and feelings. Help me, Lord, to meet my inadequacies and misdirected feelings head on with You, speaking them to You unadorned, that they might all be turned from negative feelings to positive answers. Father, thank You that I can share anything and everything with You. I love You so much!

Father, This is what I want to bring to You today:

Amen

"Be anxious for nothing, but in everything by prayer and supplication, with thanksgiving, let your requests be made known to God."
Philippians 4:6 NKJV

When God Speaks to My Heart

Day 53

Dear One,

Give all of your burdens and cares over to Me. Burdens are like dangling shoelaces…dangling cares and details of everyday life. Keep them continually tied in neat bows, lying at My feet. When you allow them to become untied and dangle in disarray, you will trip and fall over them and become entangled. My peace lies in an ordered life where focus is on Me. As long as the details of everyday life are laid before My Presence, the spirit is free to soar and fly with Me.

Walk In Peace,

Your Loving Father

Father,

Father, How can I be a better student of Your ways?

Many times You have said that my peace is the barometer by which I can judge how well I am walking in Your Presence. Whenever I feel disarray and confusion or feel weighed down by the cares and details of life, thank You for helping me to remember to quiet my heart and once again come into Your Presence, with the trust and confidence of a child. Thank You, Lord, that day by day You are teaching me to discern the difference between the important and the unnecessary.

Amen

*"Cast your burden on the LORD
and He shall sustain you…."*
Psalm 55:22 NKJV

Day 54

Dear One,

Receive your rest as one who has walked many weary miles. Don't feel guilty of spending time quietly without the pressures and tasks that will cry out to be accomplished. Let Me refresh your spirit and heal your body through this time of peaceful, refreshing solitude and rest. Rest in Me. Enjoy the quiet. Enjoy the smallest of blessings around you. Resist the temptation to lock yourself into one activity after another.

I Carry You Next To My Heart,

Your Loving Father

Father,

Seasons of change have rearranged everything I have known, but it has been a liberating process, complete and filled with Your favor. Help me to never relinquish the sweetness of our time together. I get my comfort and love from You, Father. Thank You for always being there for me.

Father, How would You like for me to enjoy my time with You today?

Amen

"Come to Me, all you who labor and are heavy laden, and I will give you rest."
Matthew 11:28 NKJV

Day 55

My Child,

Spend time with Me and let's take a progressive walk together. Now you will truly see what it really means to be free. Free of self-doubt. Pray and spend time with Me, without ceasing…that is the goal, that you might live through your spirit, not your emotions. Together we will travel the journey together and your life will become a prayer. I will become your best and most trusted friend.

Together Forever,

Your Loving Father

My Father,

Today is the first day of the rest of my life. I will spend it loving You.

How I long to know You more, day by day, in every way. I never want to be satisfied with yesterday's blessings. I want to let my heart soar in continual communion with You, keeping my eyes, ears, heart, and mind focused on You. You are my Treasure!

Amen

"Pray Without Ceasing."
2 Thessalonians 5:17 NKJV

My Precious Child,

Relax and enjoy the time that I have given to you. I will faithfully redeem your time spent with me. Come to Me with a relaxed, joyous heart. Resist the temptation to avoid time spent quietly and peacefully with Me. Times of tranquility bring peace to the spirit. Take the time to get to know Me, to share with Me your joys, and let's fellowship together. Work will always be there. If you wait until it is done to find the time for Me and My Word, you will never find the time to truly enjoy the vitality and refreshing of a walk with Me. Do not let work and responsibilities rule your time. Reach out and take My hand, letting Me direct the work, the play, and the rest.

I Love You,

Your Father

Thank You, loving Father,

For the peace Your Spirit brings. Thank You for joy and laughter and the beauty of Your creation. But most of all, thank You for the moment by moment wonderment of being Your child. Every day You surprise me anew with something to delight my soul.

Precious Father, How can I more effectively let You direct every facet of my life?

Amen

"Take My yoke upon you and learn from Me, for I am gentle and lowly in heart, and you will find rest for your souls. For My yoke is easy and My burden is light."
Matthew 11:29-30 NKJV

Day 57

My Child,

Ours is a sacred trust that can only be maintained through constant communion. Constant awareness—because when our communion together wanes, so does all else that is of importance in the life of the Spirit. Constant vigilance that secures a continual focus upon Me in worship and prayer keeps the spirit ever rising to new levels of effectiveness. Know that it is possible for the spirit and mind to be in constant prayer and worship, even while engaging in the affairs of the day. Continually strive for this. Keep your thoughts on Me, and you shall not waver or draw back. Determine your course and stick to it with diligence.

Continue On With Me,

Your Faithful Father

Dear Father,

Thank You for Your faithfulness and love in my life. When I am weary and tired, or when I am excited and feel blessed, in all circumstances I will determine with tenacity and vigilance to always be found in Your Presence, communing with You!

Amen

Father, The desire of my heart is to have a continual focus on You in worship and prayer throughout the day and night. Father, I love You! Let me count the ways:

"Continue earnestly in prayer, being vigilant in it with thanksgiving."
Colossians 4:2 NKJV

My Child,

Eye hath not seen nor ear heard the wondrous works I bring to pass for those who love Me. Don't restrain your thinking as to what you can see. Let your thinking scan the far vistas of My creative power. Handle each situation as it arises with confidence and assurance. Trust Me to make a way for each task that I lay before you. Through trust and perseverance, each task shall be completed well, and in My time. Move forward with a renewed and refreshed spirit, and be alive to My ways and leadings. Respond with alertness, trust, peace, and joy. Your days will build beautifully, one upon the other, as a patchwork quilt is sewn together to become perfect and whole. Just as each square of the quilt is different, so will each day be different, but complete in every way. Rest and be confident in My love and protection for you. Rejoice as each day unfolds to make your life whole and complete.

You Are Blessed,

Your Loving Father

Father,

Help me to always look to You, and to not make assumptions in my life. Teach me to be flexible and to release my life unto You, knowing that Your way is always best. My truest desire is to trust You with every detail of my life…to follow You with dexterity and gladness.

Father, What areas of my life do I need to hand off to You?

Amen

"A man's heart plans his way,
But the Lord directs His steps."
Proverbs 16:9 NKJV

My Precious Child,

Don't lose your strength and purpose in life by striving to be good enough…trying to be accepted. A child of God does not have to try to be good enough. He is counted as worthy because of My Son's death on the cross. This is your covering, your righteousness…your spiritual inheritance! Seek to please Me and don't be worried about the sanction or endoresement of man. Look to Me for your approval. Stand straight as an arrow looking neither to the right nor left, and walk confidently.

I Love You,

Your Father

Dear Father,

Father, I bring my insecurities to You. What areas need Your healing?

It is so easy for me to seek the approval of those around me and to forget that I have Your approval and all is well. Feeling unaccepted truly does drain my strength and turns my focus off Your Presence in my life. I know that You love me unconditionally, and take delight and joy in me. I don't have to prove anything to You, because You know and understand every facet of my being, and still, You love and treasure me. The reality of it is too wonderful for words! Thank You, Father!

Amen

*"For by grace you have been saved through faith,
and that not of yourselves; it is the gift of God,
not of works, lest anyone should boast."*
Ephesians 2:8-9 NKJV

Day 60

My Child,

Put your trust in Me. If you have done wrong, repent and go on. Forgiveness brings life. Repent and rejoice in Me. Lighten your burden by giving it to Me. Don't carry that which was not meant to be carried. If you have been hurt, give it to Me. Then, go on your way rejoicing. Love with your whole heart, free from concern, and turn the other cheek. Anger cannot feed in such an environment. It can feed upon itself but not upon you. Keep your spirit pure before Me. Do not give anger or bitterness a moment to breed.

You Are Blessed,

Your Father

Father,

Every time I am hurt because of the actions of others, help me choose to forgive, bless, and give it all to You, with no expectations. Father, the desire of my heart is to have a pure heart in all I say and do, before You.

Father, Please show me the areas of hurt and bitterness that I have hidden in my heart, which need to be brought to the light.

Amen

"Let all bitterness, wrath, anger, clamor, and evil speaking be put away from you, with all malice. And be kind to one another, tenderhearted, forgiving one another, just as God in Christ also forgave you."
Ephesians 4:31-32 NKJV

My Child,

Stand firm and tall, for you are a full-grown Oak that cannot be toppled. Let your faith be strong and sure. Stand like the Oak, feet solidly planted and arms outstretched in blessing and praise. I water and refresh the outstretched arms, and the Oak, in turn, gives blessing, shade, and refreshing to those who come within its outstretched boughs. Receiving and blessing. Receiving and blessing. The Oak in its strength is a blessing to many. So shall you be.

With Blessings,

Your Father

Dear Father,

Father, How can I bless someone today?

I will sing to You love songs with outstretched arms in thanksgiving and praise. Thank You for refreshing me and nourishing me with Your love and blessings. The joy of my heart is that You bring Your treasures to me that I might be a blessing, too.

Amen

"That they may be called trees of righteousness,
The planting of the LORD, that He may be glorified."
Isaiah 61:3 NKJV

Day 62

My Precious Child,

Look to Me and you shall not want for any good thing. My glory shall shine about you as the noonday sun. You are being established and well grounded. Your way has been predestined by Me. Walk jubilantly! Rest in My care. My generosity is infinite. Labor not to analyze each need. Leave the diagnosis and mechanics in My hand. Resist the temptation to worry or to allow the enemy to dull your faith. You *be* and I will *do*. I shall lead you! Fear not, for the foundation upon which you stand is Me! Delight this day in that very assurance.

You Are Precious To Me!

Your Loving Father

Father,

Help me to lay my cares aside and rest in Your care. Help me to love freely, with thanksgiving and a heart full of joyful praise. I will look to You in absolute trust and delight in You, Father!

Amen

Father, Show me the walls I have built around my heart that keep me from fully resting in Your care.

"The Lord is my Shepherd; I shall not want."
Psalm 23:1 NKJV

Day 63

My Child,

Worship Me in spirit and in truth, for it is through worship that real fellowship is found in Me. Worship will open up your spirit to Me. Worship takes down the walls that would keep Me out. True worship brings right standing with Me, for it breaks down every barrier and opens the door for communion and intimate fellowship. Raise up your voice in song to Me, and I shall hear and take pleasure in you. Raise up your heart in praise and sincere thanksgiving.

I Rejoice In You,

Your Loving Father

Father,

Father, How can I bless You even more as I worship You?

I long to show my love for You through ever purposeful worship. True worship is intimately loving You with all of my being. I pray that there would never be walls between us that would keep You out. Help me to simply come into Your Presence and lovingly open my heart—releasing the joy within. Thank You so much!

Amen

"…if anyone is a worshiper of God and does His will, He hears him."
John 9:31 NKJV

My Precious Child,

Sing as a bird. A bird does not sing for love and approval. He sings for the pure joy of singing, for the pure joy of being a part of My creation. My child, open your heart and sing unto Me. Sing as My songbird, for the pure joy of My love within you and for the pure joy of being Mine. That pure joy and love will pour through you, and others will seek that joy of being Mine, too. Let your songs of praise flow from your lips as a waterfall to a dry and thirsty land. In perfect trust, sing forth My praises. Take a lesson from My small-winged creation. Continually sing My praises.

Sing with Joy!

Your Loving Father

Father,

Every morning the birds sing with such pure exuberance and beauty. I can only imagine what joy we bring to Your heart when we sing praises to You! Help me to praise You with that same pure exuberance, joy, and beauty. I want to trust and delight in being Yours. I want to join the symphony of praise—all of Your creation—in singing praises to You!

Father, Please give to me a "New Song" from Your heart to sing to You today.

Amen

"I will sing to the LORD as long as I live; I will sing praise to my God while I have my being."
Psalm 104:33 NKJV

My Child,

Inner peace is brought forth through a process that must be lived step-by-step. Rejoice in the becoming. Relax and know My will for you, to have a loving and pure heart. I will show you the beauty of My Kingdom. I will show you what it means to be My disciple, steadfast, immovable, and unafraid. Remain unruffled in the shadow of My protection, for My wing shall protect you, uphold you, and show you the way. You will experience many upheavals in life, but nothing shall cause you defeat. Rest in the power of your Maker and Friend—I will bring you through, and you shall know the sweet savor of victory!

You Are Blessed,

Your Loving Father

Father,

Father, Today I place my hand in Yours with the trust of a child. What areas in my life would You have me release completely to You?

Thank You for Your faithfulness, protection, and loving care over me and those I love. Thank You for directing my every step and for the peace to know that even through the storms, You are there holding my hand and leading me through to victory. You mean everything to me, Father!

Amen

"These things I have spoken to you, that in Me you may have peace. In the world you will have tribulation; but be of good cheer, I have overcome the world."
John 16:33 NKJV

My Child,

Warmth and affection are vital to growth in My Spirit. Be an example of the warmth and love that is Me. Be not sparing. There is more than enough. Give without fear. Simply give. Giving lightens the load of your heart and makes room for receiving. My gift of love manifested in you becomes a beautiful gift as you go forth sharing it and bestowing it with ever increasing intensity and strength of purpose. Be a magnifier of My love. Give forth as I give forth, without reservation, without fear, and without thought of yourself.

Love With My Love,

Your Father

Loving Father,

Nothing is more wonderful than Your love. Thank You for Your Presence in my life, which is Your love. I want to be in Your Presence, and a carrier of Your love at all times—an expression of Your love!

Father, Who would You have me reach out to this day? Give me the right and encouraging words to say.

Amen

"This is My commandment, that you love one another as I have loved you."
John 15:12 NKJV

My Dear Child,

Carry My love forth to every cold and empty seeking heart that I lead your way. Pour forth streams of compassion and My divine love. There are so many hurting people looking for natural love that lacks warmth and life. My living, divine love brings healing and spiritual completeness to the receiver. Be a restorer of My living, eternal love. You have received; now give. Give with abundance. Give with no reservations. Give forth with exuberance. Give forth with quiet strength. Just give forth. Place your hand in Mine and give forth as you receive abundantly from Me.

Love As I Love,

Your Loving Father

Dear Father,

Father, Help me to be alert and to move when You prompt me—keeping my focus on You so that I don't let Your "Divine Appointments" pass me by.

Your love has transformed my life. What an adventure to see others' lives changed in the same way through Your Presence and the warmth and joy of Your divine love. Your love brings healing and restoration. Thank You for trusting me with Your limitless love. Show me new ways to share Your love and healing to others. I love You, Father!

Amen

"If we love one another, God abides in us, and His love has been perfected in us."
1 John 4:12 NKJV

My Child,

The race is won by those with steady persistence, not those who run in agitated spurts! Do not struggle with the whys of life. I have been with you the whole way, lighting your path with truth, and I will continue to be with you. Let that light shine in your life with brilliance. Continue straight ahead. Nothing will be lost, destroyed, or mislaid along the path. Nor shall anything be accepted that is not from Me. I have protected you and will lead you to a wide, spacious place of blessing. I have brought you through many troubled and mired waters, and yet the mire has fallen away and left only My truth and blessing.

Trust In Me!

Your Loving Father

Thank You, Father,

I do trust You to lead me, day by day, along the pathway You have chosen for me. When I struggle with the whys and uncertainties, help me choose to remember that when I trust You and persistently walk with You, Your truth and blessing always prevail in my life.

Father, I bring these areas of struggle to You, that Your truth and blessing may shine upon them and give me peace:

Amen

*"…we also glory in tribulations, knowing that
tribulation produces perseverance; and
perseverance, character; and character, hope."*

Romans 5:3-4 NKJV

My Child,

My joy is your strength and it shall continue to be. Linger over and delight in the joy I bring your way. Be as a child who handles a beautiful jewel, turning it over and over in his hand. He does not try to figure out the gem's facets, but simply revels in its timeless beauty. Be a communicator of My joy—that sparkle of life. Joy's reflection shall shine forth to others and they will be warmed by the glow. Life grows in warmth. Reflect warmth to those who are new to My love and strength to My seasoned veterans. My Word is that jewel that reflects the light and glow. Be a reflector of that light as you continually look into My Word, turning it over and over in your hand, reflecting its warmth and life-giving glow. Keep your life in the Word, and the life you pass on to others—a reflection of that Word. Magnify the Word, rejoice in the Word, and reflect the Word.

You Are Precious To Me,

Your Father

I Love You, Father!

Thank You for Your Word, Father. What would You have me learn from Your written and spoken Word today?

I love the beauty, warmth, life, and joy of Your love—of Your Word, which is You! Such joy You bring to my heart every day. Thank You for filling my heart with Your Words of love. Father, I love You!

Amen

"And Your word was to me the joy and rejoicing of my heart; For I am called by Your name."
Jeremiah 15:16 NKJV

My Child,

Light shall be the burden carried of My compassion and love. Let it flow from you as gently and easily as the breath of My Spirit. Forbearance is a virtue to be pursued and obtained. It is captured through constant and vigilant love and acceptance—unconditional love, given and received, untainted by performance orientation. Unconditional love given brings forth unconditional love received. Give it liberally and unrestricted, to the joy of your heart, and to the joy of My heart. You shall see and experience more love than you have ever known. Reach out with acceptance and love.

With Unconditional Love,

Your Father

Father,

I want to love unconditionally without thought of return, for the greatest love of all is always from YOU. Your way is wonderful and brings such joy and fulfillment. Thank You, Father, for Your love!

Father, I want to hear Your unconditional words of love to my heart today.

Amen

"Finally, all of you be of one mind, having compassion for one another; love as brothers, be tenderhearted, be courteous; not returning evil for evil or reviling for reviling, but on the contrary blessing, knowing that you were called to this, that you may inherit a blessing."
1 Peter 3:8-9 NKJV

Dear Child,

Learn to manage your emotions through forbearance. Acceptance in the midst of trials is truly taking the high road. The road is sparsely traveled but prepared for you. Follow it with diligence. Forsake resistance, apprehension, and dissatisfaction. Follow the path of discipline, diligence, and delight. Cover the lack and need of others with My love. The world waits to condemn. Reach out and instead accept, encourage, and love. Be long-suffering and patient, offering compassion, acceptance, and My love.

Accept, Encourage, And Love!

Your Loving Father

Father,

Father, When I am tempted to do or say something that is not loving or honoring, I will choose to bring blessing instead by:

I cannot earn Your love, and yet I try. Freely You give of Your love by grace, and I want to also be a giver of love and blessings, without restrictions. Help me, Father, to judge not, that I may not be judged. Thank You for helping me, by Your grace, to simply love.

Amen

"And above all things have fervent love for one another for 'love will cover a multitude of sins.'"
1 Peter 4:8 NKJV

Day 72

My Child,

In baking a cake, you add the ingredients one-by-one, mix them carefully, bake the cake, and serve it. I prepare My servants in a similar way and then serve them to the world as a sweet aroma, drawing the world to Me. Be prepared to go forth with joy, for I have divinely prepared you. I have molded and shaped you to perfection with My love. You shall bless and refresh, heal, and restore. Yours shall be the family of God!

I Love You!

Your Father

Father,

I cherish what You have done for me, day-by-day, year-by-year, adding each beautiful ingredient to my life. I see glimpses of Your plan for me coming together. I love You, Lord, with all my heart, and hunger to follow after You!

Father, How can I serve You today?

Amen

"...through love, serve one another."
Galatians 5:13 NKJV

Day 73

My Child,

Remain in My peace, no matter what the situation. My peace is like a warm blanket and is maintained through trust in Me. Fear and anxiety are the opposite of trust. Walk in peace, joy, and trust. Real love moves when the peace within says, now is the time to act. Real love is unselfish. It isn't strained and stressful. Rest in My love and My peace. Know that I am in charge and all will be well. Give freely, as I lead you to give in peace, not as pressure leads you to give through guilt. Be a giver of the strength of My Word, through peace.

Remain In My Peace!

Your Loving Father

Father,

I am seeking Your heart, that Your Word and Your peace would reside in mine. When I find myself walking in fear and anxiety, I will once again wrap myself in the warm covering of Your love and peace.

Father, How can I trust You more today?

Amen

"Trust in the LORD with all your heart, And lean not on your own understanding."
Proverbs 3:5 NKJV

My Child,

Contained within your heart is the knowledge of My love. It is a love unhindered by time and distance. It extends beyond the limited confines of the mind. It must be understood from the heart. My love is boundless. Love as I have loved you. Be My love. Manifest My love. Be a reflection of My love to others. Grow in My love day-by-day. The more you understand of My love and walk in My love, the more you can give of My love. You can only give what you have. Walk in My light that you might turn the darkness around others into light. Darkness cannot abide in the presence of My light. My light and My love are eternal.

Love As I Love,

Your Loving Father

Father,

It is so good to know I am loved by You. You love me, just because. Not because of what I can do for You or how good or holy I can be. You just love me. You bless me and give me Your best—what is uniquely best for me. Teach me to walk unafraid, confident, and secure. Give me each day Your peace and Your joy. Help my heart to trust that You are in control, working all things together for my good. Nothing will slip by You. You will always be there to help me. Thank You for loving me!

Father, Your love keeps life simple, not complex. Today and every day the desire of my heart is to love with Your love. Today I will reflect Your love by:

Amen

"He who does not love does not know God,
for God is love."
1 John 4:8 NKJV

My Child,

I am in control of your destiny, and each page of your life will turn at its appointed time. Continue to walk in My grace and extend it out to others. Grace is a treasure to be gently held in the heart and tenderly given as a gift to others, that they might receive it as a blessing and with joy. Live My love by speaking words of mercy and compassion. Speak My Word to those who are hungry and in search of hope and healing. Let it flow by the power of My Holy Spirit through you. Let the majesty of My love pour through you uncomplicated and uncontrived. Be simply the revolving door through which My love, grace, and compassion are extended to My people.

I Love You And Direct Your Paths,

Your Loving Father

Father,

Father, What words of grace and kindness would You have me to offer to someone today?

Help my words to always be those of patience, love, and grace, uncomplicated by worries or hurts. Lord, help me to avoid being tempted to worry about Your plan for my life or for others' lives. Help me to simply trust You to bring Your divine plan to pass as I fulfill my part, being Your obedient child with a joyful, trusting, and peaceful heart.

Amen

"The words of a wise man's mouth are gracious."
Ecclesiastes 10:12 NKJV

My Child,

There are all kinds of love. Love that rejoices in the accomplishments of others, love that sticks close through failure and pain, love that lifts the burden of wrongs endured, and love that persists against all odds. My Word spoken compassionately and then believed and received in the heart—this is the love I have provided you to give. Don't let up when the odds seem slim and defeat wants to prevail. Turn defeat into victory by claiming My Word and standing on that truth undaunted by the passing scene, for My Word stands and My promises are sure. Remain strong in your faith and strong in the love I have given you. Then give that love to others. Be a giver, not a taker. Offer your love to others without thought of return, taking only from Me, My love, and you will never lack.

I Love You,

Your Father

Father,

Help me to truly love unconditionally without expectations or thought of return. When tension builds with those I love, help me view the situation as an opportunity to turn things around by speaking Your Word and believing the best in my heart. You are such an awesome, powerful God, and when I stand strong, undaunted by the passing scenes of life, the outcome always strengthens my faith and love for You. Thank You for the adventure of life and Your steadfast love!

Father, Who would You have me love with Your love today?

Amen

"Love bears all things, believes all things, hopes all things, endures all things. Love never fails."
1 Corinthians 13:7-8 NKJV

My Child,

Let your life sing within the incredible beauty and flawless framework of the symphony I have created you to be. Enjoy the beauty, the perfect timing, and the music of your life that I have composed—others shall enjoy it also and be blessed. Be the symphony I have predestined you to be through confidence in Me, and by an unmovable faith that I have written the score to perfection. Blessed are the ones who allow Me to inscribe in their lives…a symphony.

Be Blessed This Day!

Your Loving Father

Father,

Father, Today I worship You and bless You with songs of praise, love, and gratefulness.

May I always allow You, Lord, to create, write, and conduct the beautiful music of my life. How wonderful to know that the composition of my life was inscribed by the Creator of the Universe. I choose to let my life sing within the perfection, beauty, and flawless timing of the symphony You have created me to be.

Amen

"Behold, My servants shall sing for joy of heart."
Isaiah 65:14 NKJV

My Child,

Regard in your heart, take notice of and pay special attention to the times and the seasons of My visitations with you. First was the planting of the seed. Then was the tender care and nourishment of the seed—I took delight in your growth. Next came the fruitfulness. Then came the pruning and the elimination of contaminants—a necessary season. A quiet season followed where you, like a tree, grew in strength and fortitude to stand tall and straight—unmoved in the storms of life. Whereas you could bear fruit before, now you can also give peace, comfort, and protection to others. But there must also be seasons of quiet…that you might draw in strength from My Son and continue to flourish full, strong, and beautiful.

Holding Your Hand As You Grow,

Your Loving Father

Father,

Thank You for Your provision, faithfulness, and gentle care every step of the way. When times become too hard to proceed, help me to look to You and remember that You are right there with me. Thank You, Father, for the pleasure of Your company throughout all the seasons of growth in my life. I love You!

Dear Father, What season of growth am I in now and would You have me proceed?

Amen

"*[Growing in grace] they shall still bring forth*
fruit in old age: they shall be full of sap
[of spiritual vitality] and [rich in the] verdure
[of trust, love, and contentment]."
Psalm 92:14 AMP

My Child,

My heart delights in you, My child. I have planted, protected, and lovingly provided for your growth and care. You have developed and matured, and together we have rejoiced as each victory has been won. I have stabilized you and brought forth from your being, gifts and attributes of My Spirit. I am well pleased with you—My creation. There is more to be added. We shall celebrate as each day brings forth new blessings and new attainment in your life!

You Are Blessed,

Your Loving Father

Father,

Father, What would you have me lay aside, that I might walk in a more abundant life?

There is such joy in discovery of the treasures You have invested within me. Gifts, talents, anointings, and blessings, so that I might fulfill Your divine purpose for my life and live triumphantly. Father, every day is an adventure with You! I love You!

Amen

"But thanks be to God, Who gives us the victory [making us conquerors] through our Lord Jesus Christ."
1 Corinthians 15:57 AMP

Day 80

My Child,

Lasting happiness is yours as you bless and comfort My people. I have led, protected, and comforted you, that you might become a resting place for others. Trials and tribulation may come, but they are an opportunity to grow in character, and then in turn to offer strength and tenderness to comfort others. Know that in troubled times I will be there to comfort and lead you out triumphantly. Likewise, comfort and disciple others, that they might look to Me and discover a victorious, more triumphant life.

Let Me Comfort You,

Your Loving Father

Father,

Through every hardship in my life You have faithfully been there to tenderly lead me to a triumphant place of strength, courage, and fulfillment. Truly that happiness is found in passing that blessing and comfort on to Your people, just as You have comforted and blessed my life.

Father, How can I bring comfort and blessing to someone today?

Amen

"Comfort, yes, comfort My people!' Says your God."
Isaiah 40:1 NKJV

Day 81

My Child,

Unmarked paths are ahead, waiting for your footsteps, ready to reveal My truth. Celebrate and be happy in the present for it is to be savored and valued. Rejoice in the past for it has brought forth the present in all its glory. The future is Mine to bring forth as I have predestined. Know that I love you and do all things well. Be assured that what I have planned is for your best fulfillment and will come forth at its appointed time. My peace and contentment I give unto you. Not as the world gives, but solid and undisturbed by places, people, or things. Place your trust in Me, I shall bring you to a continuous, sound place of My making. Release unto Me your cares for the future and live with an abundant heart!

Trust Me!

Your Loving Father

Thank You, Father,

Father, What portions of my life am I still dragging along behind me?

For teaching me that You don't look back on any part of my life with regret. You are redeeming and using every portion of it to create a beautiful picture of Your love on the canvas of my life. When I am tempted to hang onto portions of the past, worry for the future, or am frustrated with the present, help me to once again turn it all loose and look to You, for truth and peace.

Amen

"Be happy [in your faith] and rejoice and be glad, hearted continually."
1 Thessalonians 5:16 AMP

My Child,

Ministry is a gift from Me. It is to be given out of a genuine heart, for the sheer joy and pleasure of giving without agendas or expectations of return. Ministry means giving. Benevolent and compassionate giving. Give as I lead. Attend to others with My love as easily as you breathe! Unspeakable blessings you cannot even begin to conceive await the life of a giver. Every day—a gift from Heaven—an opportunity to mature and grow in My divine plan for your life. Proceed with My peace and happiness emanating from you in everything you say and do.

You Are Precious To Me,

Your Loving Father

Father,

You are precious to me, too! You have always provided for me from the abundance of Your heart. Help me to minister Your love to others, freely and easily. May I awake every morning knowing that each day is a beautiful, new opportunity from You, to be shared. And Father, may I always remember the pleasure of giving without agendas or expectations of return, simply for the pure joy of giving.

Loving Father, How would You have me share Your love today?

Amen

"It is more blessed to give than to receive."
Acts 20:35

Day 83

My Child,

Stand in the awareness of My love and protection. Remain steadfast in the knowledge of My fulfillment in your life. I shall not fail you. Be refreshed, be revived, and be at peace. Beautiful days of rejuvenation are ahead. Tucked into each day I have provided places of refreshment. Look about, and you shall see and experience My restoration on a continual basis.

I Love You,

Your Father

Father,

Father, Help me to receive Your restoration and renewal today.

I realize Your beauty and peace can be found in my life, when I slow down and look and listen—causing instant refreshment and renewal. Your love can be found in a friend's face, the song of a bird, a kind word, a hug, or a gentle touch. But most of all it is heard in the Words from Your heart to mine and in the awareness of Your Presence. Thank You for Your protection, fulfillment, and love, active in my life each and every day.

Amen

"He refreshes and restores my life."
Psalm 23:3 AMP

Day 84

My Child,

Rest in My strength and plan for your life. Keep your eyes on Me. My will shall prevail. Leave the melodramas to others. Keep things easy and unencumbered. Proceed with simplicity. Respond with clarity and go about your days with assurance. Magnify My Word and minimize problems. Spend time with Me and walk out your life undisturbed, unperturbed, and unafraid, resting in the peace and power of My love.

You Can Trust Me!

Your Father

Father,

How exciting to realize that when I rest in Your peace and keep my heart undisturbed and unencumbered, You bring forth the miraculous as I truly reside in Your Presence. What an exciting way to live, Father! I love You so much!

Father, Today I bring to You everything that causes me to feel disturbed and anxious that I might walk in Your peace and trust You!

Amen

"[Not in your own strength] for it is God Who is all the while effectually at work in you [energizing and creating in you the power and desire] both to will and to work for His good pleasure and satisfaction and delight."
Philippians 2:13 AMP

My Child,

Light the fire of joy in your heart. Light the fire of hope springing alive through peace. Ignite the fire of forgiveness and love. Allow My compassion and love to go forth from you as gently and easily as the breath of My Spirit. Go forth with joy, go forth with peace, go forth with love, go forth with the gifts of My Spirit. Stand strong and tall in My love and in standing tall, shade others with My love.

Love As I Love,

Your Father

My Father,

Father, I bring to You those who have been harder for me to love unconditionally. Please show me how You see them, so I can love them as You do.

Thank You for touching my life with such meaning and purpose. Develop within me, good and bountiful fruit, that I might bless and love others as You do. The rewards of learning to love with Your love far outweigh any struggles and bring forth the greatest joys in my life. Thank You, Lord, for trusting me to love Your treasures, Your people.

Amen

*"But the fruit of the [Holy Spirit] [the work
which His Presence within us accomplishes]
is love, joy (gladness), peace, patience
(an even temper, forbearance), kindness,
goodness, (benevolence), faithfulness."
Galatians 5:22 AMP*

My Child,

Forbearance is a virtue to be pursued and obtained. It is captured through constant and vigilant love and acceptance, unconditionally given and received. Offer it liberally and unrestricted, from the depths of your heart. You shall see and experience more blessing than you have ever known. Reach out with acceptance and compassion to others—and receive My abundant blessings for your life.

Be Loving And Patient!

Your Loving Father

Father,

You have wondrously blessed my life with opportunities to reach out and respond to others with compassion. Help me to be unafraid of repercussions, simply extending love and letting You take care of the results. Father, may I always respond to rejection or offence with Your patience and acceptance, which heals and sets us free.

Father, When I'm tempted to respond negatively help me remember how You treat me with such love and patience.

Amen

"[We pray] that you may be invigorated and strengthened with all power according to the might of His glory, [to exercise] every kind of endurance and patience (perseverance and forbearance) with joy."
Colossians 1:11 AMP

My Child,

Rejoicing in the present allows My Spirit reign in your life. Rejoicing relies on trust and faith, which are the bulwarks of My peace. No wind of trial shall diminish you or knock you over. The tempest may blow, but you shall remain firm and strong, able to withstand and remain steady. My word to you this day is, remain steadfast in My love. Wrap it around you as a cloak. Let Me handle the details. You handle the rejoicing.

You Are Loved, My Child,

Your Father

Father,

Father, I am sometimes tempted to get anxious with the events of my world. Show me ways to absolutely trust in You.

Thank You for teaching me to trust You through the many challenges of life. Help me to know that I'm always made stronger and more resolute, when I trust Your love and determine to rejoice in the present, letting Your Spirit reign. What a wonderful gift to be able to rejoice in Your peace.

Amen

"Rejoice in the Lord always [delight, gladden yourselves in Him]; again I say, Rejoice!"
Philippians 4:4 AMP

My Child,

Be mindful of My love for you and love others in the same way. Don't point out wrongs and slights. Pray. Be a praise giver, not a slight harborer. Be a restorer. Be a waterer and the bearer of blessings. Be My love and My light to others in your life. Be assured of My love for you.

Love As I Love,

Your Father

Father,

Help me reach out with love, compassion, and forgiveness. To be a source of unconditional love and encouragement. Use my words to cover lack and need with Your love. Thank You, Father, for nudging me when I start to speak negatively about one of Your treasures.

Father, Today I will focus on thinking and speaking positive words of blessing, love, and encouragement.

Amen

"Be gentle and forbearing with one another and, if one has a difference (a grievance or complaint) against another, readily pardoning each other; even as the Lord has [freely] forgiven you, so must you also [forgive]."
Colossians 3:13 AMP

My Child,

Change is not always easy, but necessary to bring forth growth. Accept change with a patient heart, welcoming it with open arms. It is your friend. When it seems that change will overwhelm you, stand back with resolute faith and trust that My hand is at work in your life. Be at peace, for I am always with you, stirring confidence within you, reassuring, directing, and loving you. I am fashioning the fabric of your life into a tight weave that not one blessing will fall through. All will come to pass at My appointed time and in My appointed way. Set your Spirit at peace and rejoice, for with My perfect timing it shall all come together— flawless and with precision. Rest in that assurance.

I Will Never Leave You Or Forsake You,

Your Father

Father,

Father, Show me the blessings of my life and raise a grateful heart within me.

When I am impatient for Your promises to be fulfilled in my life, help me stop and remember all the blessings You have bestowed upon me already. Your thoughtful, and tender love overwhelm me with their magnitude, and my heart is full of gratefulness.

Amen

"By your steadfastness and patient endurance you shall win the true life of your souls."
Luke 21:19 AMP

My Child,

Lean into Me and commit your whole being unto Me. That is called "rest." Rest from concern of things left undone. Rest from the worry of "missing it." Relax, My child, in Me, completely removed from the passing scene. My Presence shall become precious to you in new ways undreamed of. Be content in Me. Release unto Me all cares and worries. My hand is over you to prepare you for what I have preordained. All shall be accomplished in My time and at My pace. Be at peace and know Me. Tranquility of heart shall be the fruit.

Rest In Me, My Child!

Your Heavenly Father

Father,

What a wonderful place to rest, in Your own hand of protection and creation. When I become impatient, help me to remember that I am Your creation in process. Father, I long to know Your Presence in a more intimate and personal way. Help me as I learn to rest in You. I love You, Father.

Father, Today I release unto You all of the cares and worries that have kept me from resting in Your peace.

Amen

*"Therefore my heart is glad and my glory
[my inner self] rejoices; my body too shall rest
and confidently dwell in safety."*
Psalm 16:9 AMP

My Child,

It is My love that sets you at liberty to open your heart to others freely. All you have to give is My love. Set your concerns aside. There is no freedom where fear resides. Be a carrier of My perfect love which casts out fear, and opens the door to a care free heart. Perfect love displays healthy devotion, acceptance, and forgiveness. Walk in My faultless and complete love and experience a new found freedom in life.

Love As I Love,

Your Father

Father,

Father, Show me how to love those in my life — openly and completely.

Please help me to remember it doesn't matter what others do, it only matters how I respond, Help me choose to respond with compassion, love, forgiveness, patience, and blessing. When I feel afraid, Father, help me remember that Your love covers and protects me.

Amen

"There is no fear in love; but perfect love casts out fear, because fear involves torment. But he who fears has not been made perfect in love."
1 John 4:18 NKJV

Day 92

My Child,

My love for you is boundless. A faithful love, against which nothing can overcome. You will always walk above distractions when you walk in My love with a singleness of heart and mind. Trust in Me and allow My perfect, endless love to fill your life with goodness and a passion you've not known before.

Reach Out To Me With Your Whole Heart!

Your Loving Father

Father,

Thank You for helping me, day-by-day, to stand firm and fearless with strength of heart, because of my trust in Your love and faithfulness. When I feel distracted, help me once again to focus on You and listen with my Spirit to Your words of truth and love in my heart.

Father, What else is on Your heart for me to know today?

Amen

"For His mercy and loving-kindness are great toward us, and the truth and faithfulness of the Lord endure forever."
Psalm 117:2 AMP

Day 93

My Precious Child,

Rest in My love. Fear not the storms that gather, for just as surely as the clouds congregate overhead, they will be blown away. The sun will shine brightly again and the storm will have left life-giving rain to nourish My children in ways they know not of. Be refreshed each day whether the sun shines or if clouds are overhead, for either way I will bless you, and bring forth My perfect will in your life. My eye is upon you to bless you.

Rest In Me, My Child,

Your Loving Father

Father,

Father, What is on Your heart to share with me this day?

Thank You that I can trust You each moment of every day to protect me and those I love. Thank You for bringing peace to my heart, as I walk through the storms of life, held close to Your heart.

Amen

"We love Him because He first loved us."
1 John 4:19 NKJV

My Child,

I have many things to tell you, many truths for you to learn. Day-by-day I reach out to you and place a nugget of truth in your hand for you to ponder, turning it over and studying it as it molds your life. Take each nugget, and let it work it's weight in gold. Thanksgiving, praise, and time in My Presence help reveal all truth. Seek time with Me with a positive, cheerful, joyful, and open heart—and I will reveal beautiful and profound things to you that you could have never imagined.

You Are A Treasure To My Heart!

Your Loving Father

Father,

Thank You for leading my life in truth and honor—and for showing Your great desire for my life.

Father, My heart is open to You.

Amen

*"And you shall know the truth, and
the truth shall make you free."*
John 8:32 NKJV

Day 95

My Child,

My grace is yours. Come to Me and receive My mercy. Remain tender, pliable, and teachable—and you'll discover My love is vast and expansive…far greater than you could possibly imagine. It is like a pebble thrown into the water causing the ripple effect. Sow good seed for the harvest. Seed that is motivated by pure love with no agendas or motives. Extend grace and receive grace beyond anything you've known before. Receive My love into your heart and be blessed.

My Grace is Yours,

Your Loving Father

Father,

Father, I love hearing Your words to my heart.

Every day is a gift from Your heart to me. My desire is to develop into Your likeness, with no agendas, motivated by pure love, and sowing good seeds of mercy in my life. Help my life be a reflection and picture of Your grace and love. You are my greatest treasure! I love you!

Amen

"But He gives more grace. Therefore He says:
'God resists the proud, But gives grace to the humble.'"
James 4:6 NKJV

My Child,

There is a place in the Spirit where all things are made wonderfully new each day. I welcome you to come to that place as a small child entering into My Presence with wonder and delight, undaunted by the passing scene. Continue to be as that small child, without expectations, content and at peace in My Presence. My delight is in you, My child. Stay in that place with wonderment and joy, with nothing lost, but everything gained, continuing step-by-step, your destiny to be fulfilled. Rejoice in this day that I have given you and enter in My Presence with happiness and pleasure. Allow each day to become a testament of My love for you, revealing My preordained plans for your life.

I love you!

Your Father!

Father,

The joy of being Your child is beyond words—every day is a treasured gift from You. When I find myself caught up with the cares and worries of life, help me to instead think of You and regain the peace that only You can offer. I love You so much Father!

Father, Renew my heart and help me enter Your Presence with the trust and hope of a child.

Amen

"Assuredly, I say to you, whoever does not receive the kingdom of God as a little child will by no means enter it."
Luke 18:17 NKJV

My Child,

Security comes by knowing and trusting Me. I will never fail you, but will protect you. Plan in your heart to remain secure in this place of tremendous grace. Purpose in your heart to know that I, Your loving Father will not let you down. Resolve to be at peace in this place of refuge with me. Conflict is the signal to come into My Presence, into the safety of My love, to diffuse the struggle, and bring a calm peace back into your life. It is a moment by moment decision to enter into My peace and have personal fellowship with Me.

You Are Secure In Me,

Your Loving Father

Father,

The desire of my heart is to always remember to start the day in Your Presence. To moment by moment, spend the rest of the day in fellowship with You, listening to Your instructions and sharing my heart with You. At the end of each day, show me how to go over the details of my day with You and to seek Your wisdom and understanding of what has transpired.

Father, Today I plan to stay in the peace of Your Presence, trusting the safety of Your love. My heart is listening for Your voice:

Amen

"Keep and protect me, O God, for in You I have found refuge, and in You do I put my trust and hide myself."

Psalm 16:1 AMP

My Child,

You are safe and secure in My arms of love. Depend on Me for your every breath and all that pertains to your life. I have lavished My love and favor upon you as a doting father lavishes his love and provision upon his favored child. Every moment of every day is an opportunity to partake in a banquet of love, peace, and joy with your Father and Friend. The freedom of My heart is yours. Let go of preconceived ideas and walk out your life unfettered by the past and its inconsistencies. My heart is with you to rejoice in the now. It contains all you will need for the journey to come. Run with abandon! Live with uncontained joy! Walk out each day of your life with the knowledge of My love!

I Am Your Faithful Friend.

Your Loving Father

Father,

Thank You for helping me to lay down all preconceived ideas, hurts, disappointments, and inconsistencies from the past, so that You are free to create in my life, a beautiful symphony of Your love. Thank You Father, for helping me to live in the present, and to leave the past behind in peace. I love being Your child, Father!

Father, Is there anything from the past, that I am still hanging on to?

Amen

"In You, O Lord, do I put my trust and seek refuge;"
Psalm 31:1 AMP

When God Speaks to My Heart

Day 99

My Child,

You have been through many storms that have touched areas of your life—leaving debris and disruption. Restoration and cleanup is a step-by-step endeavor. Recognizing the areas needing attention is the beginning of reconciliation and order. Don't fear the storms of life. My grace is there to protect and restore. All that is needed is a willing heart. Seek Me in every word you speak, in every thought you make, and in every action you take. I am with you in everything you do, say, feel, and think. You are never alone. Relax in My love. I will always guide your way.

I Am Always With You,

Your Father

Father,

Father, How can I look to You today and trust You more?

Thank You for Your protection, provision, and Presence in my life. Thank You, Father, that each time I come out of a storm, I find myself stronger, more grateful for Your love, and trusting You more. It is so great to know that I am never alone. I love You!

Amen

"Yes, though I walk through the [deep, sunless] valley of the shadow of death, I will fear or dread no evil, for You are with me."

Psalm 23:4 AMP

Day 100

My Child,

There are many areas in My world that need My Spirit of love and deliverance. I have placed you in positions to offer My love, which delivers. Don't hold back. Let My love flow unhindered. Let it pour out liberally that I might use it to bring freedom to those around you. Give My love as naturally as you breathe—that along with compassion will restore My people, as they begin to look toward Me.

Love As I Love You,

Your Loving Father

Father,

What an adventure it is each day, seeing how Your love delivers and restores. Help me to remember it is not about me; it's about Your love and compassion for Your people. Show me ways that I too can love others, as You do.

Father, Are there any issues in my life that are holding me back from loving others?

Amen

"Just as I have loved you, so you too should love one another."'
John 13:34 AMP

My Child,

Live your life with freedom! The vastness of My universe is yours to enjoy. There is strength in My freedom. Let My Spirit bring liberty to your heart—freedom to love, freedom to rejoice, freedom to receive My Words of life, freedom to walk in faith and trust, freedom to thank Me in all things, and freedom to *be* all that I have created you to be. Stay close to My heart, My child, and let Me continue to help you walk in the glory of My freedom.

Be Free, My Child,

Your Loving Father

Father,

Father, What cares do I need to cast aside to walk in absolute freedom with You?

Remind me to fly carefree. My goal is to walk each day without worry every day with You, Father, in the glory of Your Presence, letting the freedom of Your Spirit ring in my heart with great abounding joy. I love You so much, Father!

Amen

"Stand fast therefore in the liberty by which Christ has made us free, and do not be entangled again with a yoke of bondage."
Galatians 5:1 NKJV

My Child,

Lay down your abilities before Me and let Me develop them to their fullest. I shall increase and shape your talents. There shall be no limits put upon My assigned blessings and the use of your gifts. Let Me utilize them for My glory, and I will bring forth an abundant harvest from each talent at the appointed time and place. Remain under the constant care and abiding love of My outspread wing of protection and direction. Fear not, for life is in My safe keeping. Let Me lead the way and bring forth an abundantly blessed life for you.

Trust My Love,

Your Father

Father,

Knowing that You direct the times and seasons of my life, and open the doors of opportunity along the way, brings such peace to my heart. When I look back over my life, I can see Your hand of direction and blessing throughout each and every step. Thank You for guiding and directing my life.

Father, I lay before You my impatience in the following areas of my life that You might develop me to my best potential.

Amen

"My times are in Your hands;"
Psalm 31:15 AMP

My Child,

Stand straight and tall and be a sturdy ambassador of My Kingdom—undaunted by unloveliness or criticism—for I guide your ship. I set the sails that propel you along, and I set the boundaries. You answer to Me and Me alone, and I have set your course for victory and blessing; blessings for you and for those whose lives you touch. Be flexible and resilient in My hands, and watch Me bring forth a beautiful life—yours! Be a beacon light of love, compassion, and gentleness, with a forgiving, spacious spirit, and a light and joyous heart.

You Are My Treasure,

Your Loving Father

Father,

Father, I love the sound of Your voice, and Your Words teaching my heart to trust You completely.

You have always been there to guide my way in life—providing the answers for every question. Your steadfast love has touched my life in a beautiful way. I want to be totally secure in Your love. Show me the way to complete trust in You.

Amen

"...stand fast in the Lord, beloved."
Philippians 4:1 NKJV

My Child,

I have been listening and I love you. Know that with My love, your life has incredible potential. Release your cares to Me and know I have heard your words to Me in the night. My love and power are unhampered by tradition. Victory is just around the corner. Realms of freedom await you. Go to it, My child, for I am with you to direct your steps. I have received your words in prayer to Me and cherish these sweet moments together.

I Am With You,

Your Loving Father

Father,

Nothing is more rewarding in life than loving You, and having intimate fellowship with You. Thank You, Father, for hearing the words and passions of my heart.

Father, Thank You for spending time with me today.

Amen

*"The Lord has heard my supplication;
the Lord receives my prayer."*
Psalm 6:9 AMP

My Child,

As you encourage others, there is an enlargement of their vision and scope. It empowers them to see beyond pain and discouragement, beyond their limited sight. I have broadened your scope and brought you from a place of limited vision to see the pain in others beyond their pleasant exterior. Many cross your path who have need of love and encouragement. Watch for them as I bring them your way; you shall know, and discern, and show them the way to freedom! Be an encourager and release others into lives of potential and victory. Lead them to Me through love and compassion.

I Love You, My Child,

Your Father

Father,

Father, Who can I reach out to this day with Your words of encouragement and compassion?

You have set me free in the most miraculous and wonderful ways, and I will be eternally grateful. What joy to be a part of leading others to You and into that same amazing and incredible freedom. It is so exciting to be able to uplift and love others in the same way that You have encouraged and loved me. I love You!

Amen

*"that their hearts may be encouraged,
being knit to together in love."*
Colossians 2:2 NKJV

Day 106

My Child,

Truth is your friend and protector. Fear not, but continue to live out your life undaunted and unafraid, gleaning truth from every vantage point. Keep a watch upon your mouth to speak the truth in love, compassion, and forbearance, void of guile, resentment, or bitterness. Speak the positive in truth and love.

Be My Love,

Your Loving Father

Father,

Help me always live my life uprightly and truthfully. The desire of my heart is that my words always carry Your Spirit of truth and love.

Father, How can I please You today in word, thought, and action?

Amen

"...let our lives lovingly express truth [in all things,
speaking truly, dealing truly, living truly]."
Ephesians 4:15 AMP

When God Speaks to My Heart

My Child,

Worship allows My heart to capture your heart. Freedom is a state of mind loosed by the heart focused on Me in unrestricted worship. Don't be weighed down with daily concerns. Move through them, noticing only long enough to lift them up to Me. Let your care be in seeking freedom through intimacy with Me. The worry will melt away and your needs will be met in the power of My Presence. Heaviness will fall away in the absolute beauty and sincerity of My Presence.

Look To Me,

Your Father

Precious Father,

Dear Father, Please teach me how to hand my cares over to You…and to worship You with all of my heart.

You have captured my heart! I long to come into greater depths of intimately loving You through the freedom of worship. Through worship my whole being sings and celebrates the joy of loving You!

Amen

"O worship the Lord in the beauty of holiness;"
Psalm 96:9 AMP

Day 108

My Child,

Allow your heaviness of heart to be replaced by My pure joy, fashioned in My purifying fire. It shall come forth resounding within My power and grace, and you shall rise up and sing. My power, authority, and healing are there for you when you are weary from the battle. You shall recognize My renewing gifts, because you have been through the fire and are coming through with fine-tuned brilliance upon you. Don't worry over the distant smoke. See the brilliance of My light. Dance in the midst of My refining fire.

Dance And Sing, My Child!

Your Loving Father

Father,

I thank You that the spirit of heaviness is being replaced by Your pure joy. What a pleasure to recognize the transformation of my life. Help me to look to Your power, authority, and healing when I am weary from life's battle, that I might come through with the brilliance of Your Spirit upon me.

Father, You make my heart sing with pure joy. How can I bring joy to Your heart today?

Amen

"For He is like a refiner's fire…"
Malachi 3:2 AMP

My Child,

Lift up your faith to Me. Remain steadfast and trust in My promises to you. Enter into fellowship with Me through worship and praise and an open heart. Release your heart to Me, completely. It is there that My Holy Spirit makes you entire and whole.

You Are Blessed,

Your Loving Father

Dearest Father,

Father, How can I be more open to Your loving Presence in my life?

My desire is to spend every waking and sleeping hour in Your Holy Presence, that place of intimate fellowship with You. Thank You for the beauty of Your Presence in my life.

Amen

*"O God, my heart is fixed
(steadfast, in the confidence of faith);"*
Psalm 108:1 AMP

My Child,

I am the beautiful, glistening light of the world. Allow My radiance to shine bright in your life—others will be drawn to the light of My Presence. It will reflect onto their faces. They won't see that reflection happening, but it will because it is My light and My Presence, and it is doing what I sent it forth to do. By sharing compassion and My love to others, you are holding My Presence, offering My light and restoration. Simply be the reflection of My love, and I will do what needs to be done in the hearts of others.

You Are Blessed,

Your Loving Father

My Father,

Help place a love in my heart for Your people—that I might please You by touching others with Your hope, joy, and restoring light. Thank You, Father!

Father, What is on Your heart for me to hear today?

Amen

"There it was—the true Light was then coming into the world [the genuine, perfect, steadfast Light] that illumines every person."
John 1:9 AMP

My Child,

Be a portrait of My faithfulness and love. Let Me paint the picture clearly and beautifully in your life. Vivid, wonderful colors for all to see—a portrait of Me, seen through My faithfulness without limit, My love to impart, into the niches and crevices of each aching heart. Be diligent, be faithful. My glory you will see, as you minister My love to every need.

Be My Love,

Your Father

Father,

Every day that goes by, Your love becomes more precious to me. Every day that goes by brings a deeper appreciation for Your faithfulness in my life. Thank You, Father, for sharing with me such wonderful gifts of love.

Above all, Father, You are my treasure! How can I walk closer to Your heart today?

Amen

"I have proclaimed Your faithfulness and Your salvation. I have not hid away Your steadfast love and Your truth from the great assembly."
Psalm 40:10 AMP

My Beloved Child,

Lavish adoration is what I desire from you. Come to Me in intimacy. Worship by the Spirit brings life. Exaltation brings My glory, My Presence, and My goodness. Be a carrier of intimate worship, praise, thanksgiving, and intimacy with Me, through your steadfast love, faithfulness, and grace extended to others in the light of My love. Worship Me and experience true freedom—rare and beautiful to behold.

You Are Blessed,

Your Loving Father

Father,

Your steadfast love, faithfulness, and goodness daily bring such joy to my heart. Thank You, Father, that You not only love me with an unfathomable love, but that You also encircle me with a family of friends who love me. Your ways are so wonderful to me!

Father, Speak to my heart that I might further learn Your ways.

Amen

"'God is a Spirit (a spiritual Being) and those who worship Him must worship Him in spirit and in truth (reality).'"
John 4:24 AMP

My Precious Child,

A greater destiny awaits you. You are My child, and I love you—all I have is yours. My blessing and favor are upon you. They are all yours, My child, and your potential is endless. See the past merge into the present with peace and favor. See My light rest upon you to accomplish all I set before you. The ministry of grace has filled your life and placed you on solid footing for the things to come. You will not miss the divine plan for your life. It is yours to explore and take delight in with all your heart.

I Love You!

Your Father

Father,

Thank You, Father, for giving me a sense of my destiny, and I look to You for my future.

You have said that I will not miss the wondrous things You have in store for me, if I keep my trust in You. Father, help me to have faith that no matter how things look, I can trust You. Thank You, Father, for merging the past into the present with peace and favor, and for blessing my future with Your guiding hand. I love You!

Amen

"You have granted me life and favor,
...and Your care has preserved my spirit."
Job 10:12 NKJV

My Child,

I have a plan for your life. Know that within My framework of time, much has been accomplished and much shall stand the passage of time. Each day is a composition—compiling a masterpiece of great beauty. Continue on in pursuit of your personal best and My divine plan for your life. Run undaunted for the gold, and know this: the quest is worth every effort. You are surrounded by My authority and strength as you run.

I Am Proud Of You, My Child,

Your Loving Father

Loving Father,

Thank You for teaching me that every day is complete in You. That at the end of the day, I can go to sleep with peace, knowing that another portion of Your masterpiece has been completed in my life, because You lead, guide, and direct my steps.

Father, Am I on course regarding Your plans for my life?

Amen

*"Let us run with patient endurance and steady
and active persistence, the appointed
course of the race, that is set before us."*
Hebrews 12:1 AMP

My Child,

You are a sweet fragrance unto Me. Treasure the peace of the hour. Continue our moments spent together, ever mindful of My unconditional love for you. Pour it out onto others. Be strengthened this day. Continue forward with renewed vision and strength and be blessed. You have come a long way. Bask this day in the warmth and aroma of My love.

You Bring Me Joy,

Your Loving Father

Father,

Father, How can I be a beautiful fragrance unto You today?

Your words of encouragement and unconditional love give me strength to go forward, knowing that You are always with me for every challenge that comes my way. Thank You for that assurance. I love You, Father!

Amen

"For we are the sweet fragrance of Christ [which exhales] unto God."
2 Corinthians 2:15 AMP

My Child,

Stay close to My heart and let Me know your deepest desires. Mighty and tremendous are the plans I have for you. Don't worry about what you cannot see. It is My greatest desire to bless your life with good things. I am directing your every step, making sure every detail is completely in tune. Seek My face each day. Let Me lead your way. Stay close to My heart. Let Me be a part of every thought and action as each and every day brings you closer to your heart's desires.

You Are Loved,

Your Father

Father,

I pray that I would grow closer to Your heart, and not get caught up in the events of the day and miss the Words that You would say to my heart. I don't want to miss a single Word of direction, instruction, love, encouragement, friendship, or fellowship. I love You, Father, so much!

Father, Please speak to my heart, as I share my heart with You.

Amen

"Ask, and it will be given to you; seek, and you will find; knock, and it will be opened to you."
Matthew 7:7 NKJV

My Child,

Your joy in Me is your strength and your song, your protection all the day long. Never despair! Never give up! For I see the end from the beginning, bathed in the light of My love. Victory shines forth brilliantly in My eyes. Share the knowledge of that triumph in Me, for it is yours to partake in all its fullness. The choice is always yours. Rejoice and be glad, for I have told you the outcome is success! Bask in the light of My love. It brings joy. Go forth singing, laughing, praising, rejoicing, and standing on My Word of victory.

Walk In The Joy Of My Love!

Your Loving Father

Father,

Father, You establish strength in my life with such joy. Let me count the ways:

Show me new ways to sing, laugh, praise, and rejoice in You. Help me to avoid allowing the negative emotions to creep in. I don't want to lose sight of Your vision and victory for my life. I delight in You, Father!

Amen

"The joy of the LORD is your strength."
Nehemiah 8:10 NKJV

Day 118

My Child,

Many times you have stood in the gap, being a bridge, drawing those from a place of distance to the light and truth of My love. A bridge does not take on the characteristics of those who pass over it, but of the One who created it. Continue to look to Me, your Creator, for your truth and your very being. Freely give of the love and faithfulness I have given you. Be My love to My people, and I'll do within them what needs to be done. With faith and trust in Me, you simply love!

Love As I Love You,

Your Loving Father

Father,

Help me to lovingly speak Your Words of encouragement and truth to others as You work miracles in their lives. Father, when society judges, condemns, and rejects others as unworthy, help me to remain aware that they, too, need to be loved so that You can work Your miracles in their lives. Show me new ways to love and encourage others—being a bridge to You.

Father, Teach me even more how to walk in absolute compassion.

Amen

"Walk in love, [esteeming and delighting in one another] as Christ loved us and gave Himself up for us,"
Ephesians 5:2 AMP

My Child,

Be My love! Manifest My mercy! Be a reflection of My compassion to others! Radiate My tenderness! Be a transmitter of My grace! By My Spirit be a life-giver. Stand in the gap for My precious ones. Let them learn by example. Grow in My love day-by-day. The more you understand and walk in My love, the more you can give it. You can only give what you have.

Love As I Love You,

Your Loving Father

Father,

Father, What would You have me learn today from Your heart of love?

Your love is straightforward and honest; it gives wisdom, discernment, knowledge, warmth, comfort, and truth. It restores and blesses. Your love keeps life simple, not complex. It turns darkness into light. Your love puts people on solid ground, for they know they are accepted and acceptable. This is how I want to love also, Father. Thank You for teaching me Your ways.

Amen

*"And may the Lord make you to increase and
excel and overflow in love for one another and
for all people, just as we also do for you."*
1 Thessalonians 3:12 AMP

My Child,

My Word penetrates deeply into the inner being, bringing about results of My making. My Word molds, shapes, and produces fruit that is sweet to the taste, giving life, stamina, and hope to those languishing on the sidelines. Let My Word bubble forth with abundant life to your heart. Hearken to the sound of My voice in the still of the night, in the evening hours, in the cool of the day, and in the midst of your daily activities. Tune your heart to listen, to establish unhindered communication between Me and thee. My Spirit waits for an invitation to commune.

Listen With Your Heart, My Child,

Your Loving Father

Father,

Your written Word and Your spoken Word are both such treasures to my heart. They are the foundation of everything worthwhile in life, bringing understanding, hope, and abundant life everlasting. Such a sense of destiny pervades my spirit, as I walk with You, loving Father!

Thank You, Father, for speaking words of wisdom to me today, through Your written and spoken Words.

Amen

"For the Word that God speaks is alive and full of power [making it active, operative, energizing, and effective]; it is sharper than any two-edged sword, penetrating to the dividing line of the breath of life (soul) and [the immortal] Spirit."
Hebrews 4:12 AMP

My Child,

Offer My peace and love to others as I have given My love and peace to you. See others through My eyes. Let Me love them through you, judging not, but accepting them absolutely. Accept and love them where they are. My peace I give to you that you might love without condemnation, or reservation.

I Love You!

Your Father

Father,

Loving Father, Who can I reach out to this day?

Thank You for helping me to love others unconditionally, as You love, with faithfulness and forgiveness. Father, I am so grateful to You, that as I am learning to love with Your love, You fill my life with friends who are learning to love in the same way. Father, You are so wonderful!

Amen

"Now the fruit of righteousness is sown in peace by those who make peace."
James 3:18 NKJV

My Child,

Rest in the glory of My Presence. Don't allow yourself to be weighed down by discouragement. Be free through song and worship—soar in the high places with Me. Soar high and let Me soothe your frayed wings that have been battered by the unabated winds. Have confidence, My child. Trust in Me. Love, faith, and honor are the building blocks of the spirit. All are given by My hand to be received by you. Have confidence in Me that I will bring your life to a place of triumph. Walk, run—soar with confidence.

Trust Me, My Child,

Rest In Me

Faithful Father,

Once again I put my life in Your hands, knowing that I can trust You completely. You are free to direct my feet in the way You have chosen for me to go. As I seek the answers from You, You bring all good things to my life, so that I can live abundantly.

Father, Am I following the path You would have me follow?

Amen

"Now to Him who is able to keep you from stumbling,
and to make you stand in the presence of
His glory blameless with great joy,"
Jude 24 NASB

Day 123

My Child,

Fill your life with song. Come into My Presence with singing. Glorious and magnificent praise brings joy and abundant life to My children—especially to those who languish in the heat of battle. Restrain not the sound of worship in your heart. Let it resonate with glorious abandon. Let My peace reign in your heart, as I replace disappointment and uncertainty with happiness and reassurance, as you lift your praises to Me. Go forth now, unencumbered. Carry on, facing life straight ahead in trust and faith that what I have begun in you, I will complete. I will never abandon you. You are protected within My constant care. Forget the past and what you have seen as failure because all I see is growth. Let the past go, for I am quick to restore and hasten to lift you up when you lose your footing. Hold your head up high—in confidence.

I Will Never Leave You Or Forsake You,

Your Loving Father

Father,

Loving Father, I will come into Your Presence with singing this day.

Thank You for Your constant, unfailing care. It is so wonderful to know that what I see as failure, You see as growth. Help me to live in absolute trust and faith in You, with a knowing that what You have begun in my life, You will complete! Show me how to lift my heart in praise to You, Father.

Amen

"Speak out to one another in psalms and hymns and spiritual songs, offering praise with voices [and instruments] and making melody with all your heart to the Lord."
Ephesians 5:19 AMP

My Child,

Amongst My flowers may grow thorns, but they cannot affect the beauty and blessing of those flowers. For My sun, rain, and soil cause them to flourish, grow, and shine forth My glory. Trust Me to continue to nourish, love, and protect you, causing you to grow and flourish. Keep your face raised toward My smile and soak up the rays of the Son. Let the rain of My Spirit refresh you and the soil of My love enfold you, causing you to thrive, strengthen, and prosper. Be at rest—My blessings for your life are near.

I Care For You,

Your Loving Father

Loving Father,

You take such good care of me. The wonder of it all is how You delight in me. Please make Your Presence more evident in my life. I am so grateful! You truly nourish, love, and protect me, causing me to thrive and grow. Thank You for Your abundant, continual blessings.

Loving Father, You have blessed my life with so many good things. I am thankful for:

Amen

"...there shall be showers of blessing
[of good, insured by God's favor]."
Ezekiel 34:26 AMP

My Child,

Stand guard at the doorway of your heart. Be aware and alert to the attitudes of pride and self-pity that will try to creep in the back door from feelings of offense and injustice. Let it not be said that you became an accuser. Let it be said that you held steady and firm to the end, extending a gracious heart of friendship and love. Straightforward and full of truth and discernment you shall be, with no hint of condemnation or struggle. It will be in My strength, brought forth from My heart, My truth, and My Word, establishing a clear, pure heart. So shall it be. Go forth with confidence, for I go before you, preparing the ground, to bring forth restoration and peace.

Love As I Love,

Your Loving Father

Father,

Father, What areas of my life have I not totally given over to You, for Your healing and restoration?

Thank You for enriching my life with meaningful and healthy relationships. Help me to maintain a clean, pure heart without finding fault, no matter how things may appear to be. Show me how to be straightforward, full of truth and discernment, and yet loving without condemnation, offense, pride, or self-pity.

Amen

"Create me a clean heart, O God, and renew a right,
persevering, and steadfast spirit within me."
Psalm 51:10 AMP

Day 126

My Child,

Lighten your heart. It need not be that heavy. I have said, "Light is the load of those who follow after Me." Set your eyes on Me. Walk in My fulfillment and peace. My children walk in the confidence of My love for them. That is where their strength and resilience come from. The promise of that love will move you through the storms of life unscathed. Nothing can penetrate the peace and joy of My Spirit. All is well. Go forth this day with gladness and strength in your heart, for I love you with a perfect and everlasting love.

You Are Blessed,

Your Father

Precious Father,

Forgive me for allowing fear and doubt to creep in. Help me to trust Your perfect love and peace which are always readily available to me. When the load seems too heavy, help me to remember where my strength and resilience come from, and to once again trust in Your magnificent and faithful love.

Dear Father, Today I choose to release my heavy heart into Your Presence with faith.

Amen

"Surely or only goodness, mercy, and unfailing love shall follow me all the days of my life,"
Psalm 23:6 AMP

When God Speaks to My Heart

My Precious One,

I am your protector and will carry you through the hard times as a trusted companion. Continue stepping out as never before, walking through each open door prepared for you. Reach out for your destiny. Grasp it with both hands. Remain undaunted and steadfast. Now you shall enjoy My many blessings and truly you will never be the same. With great hope you have endured year after year—with a resounding courage. It has been no small feat and I am so proud of you. Continue on with confidence and courage!

I Love You!

Your Proud Father

Loving Father,

Faithful Father, Help me to understand more clearly Your purpose and design for my life.

Thank You for filling my heart with expectation, courage, and resolute determination that I might live out Your promises and intended destiny for my life. Please give me the gift of childlike faith to trust and believe, without faltering, in the promises of Your Word. When I become discouraged and worn, please encourage my heart. And today, I ask for added strength and resilience as I walk toward the fulfillment of Your promises to me.

Amen

"For I will surely deliver you and you will not fall by the sword but your life will be as a reward of battle to you because you have put your trust in Me says the Lord."
Jeremiah 39:18 AMP

My Child,

Many times I have protected you in life. Fear not the challenges that come. They cannot harm you. I shall lead and guide you. Be strong and confident—let Me show you greater levels of faith and trust. Continue on with dedication and commitment to your faith. Trust in Me as your support. You will encounter demanding and tough situations, but together we shall be triumphant and make greater strides—more than ever before. Blessed assurance is the key. Bravely, declare your confidence in My ability to bring you through to victory and fulfillment.

You Are Blessed,

Your Loving Father

Thank You, Father,

For gently guiding and teaching me, day-by-day. You have always supported me as I've encountered difficult situations, teaching me how to walk life out confidently and bravely. Walking with You, Father, is walking in the miraculous. Thank You for taking me to greater strides in my growth than ever before, and for knowing that together we shall always come out triumphant.

Teach me, Father, to hear Your voice more clearly, that I might walk more confidently in life.

Amen

"For I the Lord your God hold your right hand; I am the Lord, Who says to you, Fear not; I will help you!"
Isaiah 41:13 AMP

My Child,

You will strengthen and flourish as you take in My Word, written and spoken, and stand in faith. Trust in My Word of truth; My love will cultivate and support you. Be like that beautiful, healthy tree of My choosing, and I shall make of you a tree vigorous and full of splendor—that cannot be toppled or harmed. Be My tree of righteousness, the planting of the Lord. I will care for you, cultivate and sustain you. Grow, thrive, and rejoice evermore!

Grow And Be Strong,

Your Loving Father

Dear Lord,

Father, Today I desire to grow strong and sturdy in Your love for me.

You have loved and blessed me beyond measure! Your Word brings me joy and freedom. It has caused me to grow and thrive. You surround me with pleasure and favor. I love You so much, and am so grateful!

Amen

"And he shall be like a tree firmly planted [and tended] by the streams of water, ready to bring forth its fruit in its season; its leaf also shall not fade or wither; and everything he does shall prosper [and come to maturity]."
Psalm 1:3 AMP

My Child,

Let the light of My countenance shine upon you from this day forward, undiminished by disappointment or discouragement. Focus today on the joy of My Presence, the promises I have made to you, and the song of love that My Spirit sings to you. Let it rise up strongly in your life unabated. Discard your grief and regret. Walk before Me with an upright, clean heart, with hope and trust in My sustaining love. Stand before Me confident that I will uphold you, encourage you, and bring you through to a place of victory.

I Sing Over You With Love!

Your Father

I Love You, Father,

You are the joy of my life. You bring songs of hope and love to my heart. There is such peace in Your Presence. It is there that I am able to discard all discouragement and disappointment. Every day is a new beginning and a new adventure with You!

Father, My heart reaches out to You today.

Amen

"Blessed are the people who know the joyful sound!
They walk, O LORD, in the light of Your countenance."
Psalm 89:15 NKJV

Day 131

My Child,

Allow My light to radiate through you in greater ways toward others. I have revealed to you many truths, truths that have brought freedom and light to your life. Share that light in your life, and it will make your pathway even more vivid. I have blessed you with many opportunities, designed to lead you ever closer to My heart. Narrow is the path, but wide is My love for you. Walk in the expansion of My love, and follow the destiny I have designed for your pleasure.

You Are Loved,

Your Father

Precious Father,

Father, Who can I share a small kindness with today? Give me the encouraging words to say and thus share Your tremendous grace.

Every day, the wonderment of Your love becomes more real to my heart. Just knowing that as I walk in the awesome love You have for me…You keep me on the path of Your will and Your way, bring purpose and meaning to my life. I love You, Father, so very much!

Amen

"No one after lighting a lamp puts it in a cellar,
but on the lampstand so that those
who enter may see the light."
Luke 11:33 NRSV

Day 132

My Child,

Remain steadfast for I have not stopped working in your life. I shall continue to bring forth blessings and solutions to the challenges that seem to loom and extract the peace from your life. I am the problem solver, and I have placed you where I want you to be, in order to confirm and bring forth My preordained plan for your life. Praise continues to be your safeguard, and peace is to be the barometer of your walk with Me. Continue on in strength, fortitude, and determination to see My blessing brought forth in your life. Don't worry for the future. Simply trust Me each day. Rejoice in the present and My care for you and those you love. Your pathway is abounding with My light. You will not stumble or fall. My Spirit of love shall continue to uphold, sustain, train, and guide you.

I Love You, My Child,

Your Father

I Love You, Father!

When I simply trust You for today, You always bring forth the answers for tomorrow. Help me when I am tempted to worry about the future, to remember that You hold me in the palm of Your hand, and that You have a plan for my life. Thank You, Father, for continuing to remind me that praise is my safeguard, and peace continues to be the barometer of my walk with You. You are my life!

Father, I am thankful that I can place my confidence in You.

Amen

"And they who know Your name [who have experience and acquaintance with Your mercy] will lean on and confidently put their trust in You,"
Psalm 9:10 AMP

Day 133

My Child,

Everything I have is yours! My love, blessing, and acceptance. Walk in confidence and poise brought forth by a total understanding of My approval and favor upon you. Know My heart and receive your inheritance and every treasure, secured for you from the foundation of the earth. Don't walk around it, beside it, or past it—instead, walk in full acceptance, trust, and full receivership of My love, blessings, acceptance, and inheritance.

Walk Fully In My Blessings For You,

Your Loving Father

Thank You, Father,

Loving Father, Thank You for the many blessings that are mine as a birthright, because I am Your child.

For Your unconditional love! Thank You that when I am tempted to feel insecure or to allow intimidation to enter my life, that You remind me that I am secure in You. I want to walk in Your acceptance, love, blessings, and full inheritance as Your child.

Amen

"Come, you that are blessed by my Father,
inherit the kingdom prepared for you from
the foundation of the world."
Matthew 25:34 NRSV

My Precious Child,

Straight into My Presence you have come, not worried or concerned with what you have done. But knowing full well, My love covers you and protects you in all that you do. Straight into My embrace you continue to come, longing to hear the Words from My heart about everything concerning your life. Know always that I will comfort you and impart Words of wisdom, commitment, and discernment. In My arms of love you have found a sanctuary of peace. My child, now listen to My heart this day and you will find the secret to make the enemy flee. Begin asking and expecting My heart to reveal the answers you seek. It's the adventure of a lifetime as you continue to search, and to be led by Me.

I Love You, My Child,

Your Loving Father

Loving Father,

Just saying Your name causes my whole being to come to rest and peace. It's true, I long to hear Your Words of life to my heart. Thank You, Father, for the privilege to approach You with confidence.

Amen

Father, Today I want to ask You about:

"We love Him, because He first loved us."
1 John 4:19 AMP

Day 135

My child,

Listen closely! I am your friend and will continue to be until the end. Don't worry about the how, when, or where. Just know I will continue to be there with you, every step of the way. Rest My embrace and continue to know it is already done, to My glory and to your delight. Every day is a treasure to be captured. You will continue to know day-by-day, My heart and My ways for you, in all that you do, for you have taken a stand to trust, believe, and freely receive My Spirit of love as a part of everything you think, do, and say.

You Are My Treasure,

Your Loving Father

Father,

Father, I will let go of these cares today and walk in complete trust.

It is amazing how things seem to fall into place when I trust in You. When I am tempted to race ahead instead of peacefully living one day at a time, help lead me with Your perfect timing. Thank You, Father, for patiently teaching me how to slow down and trust in Your plan for my life.

Amen

"So don't be anxious about tomorrow. God will take care of your tomorrow too. Live one day at a time."
Matthew 6:34 TLB

My Child,

Love and treasure those I have placed in your life. Care for and love them as I have loved you. Lighten the load of others. Minister My love to them. Moment-by-moment, day-by-day, the Word of the Lord shall be with you, bringing comfort, guidance, and peace. Bask in the goodness of My love for you. Be immersed in it with joy and share it with others. Magnificent days lie ahead. Share the blessing and rejoice — My strength and purpose you shall see.

Love As I Love,

Your Father

Precious Father,

Show me how to love and minister to those You have placed in my life. I want to be a part of Your divine plan. Thank You, Father, for letting us be an integral part of Your healing love upon the earth!

Father, Give me creative ideas and show me how to reach out to someone today.

Amen

"Love each other with brotherly affection and take delight in honoring each other."
Romans 12:10 TLB

My Child,

It is My pleasure to see you grow and develop. Don't be concerned with others' expectations of you. You are still to love each one, where they are. Step up to the challenge. Don't hesitate. Simply see them as My treasures and love them as I do—with all your might. Do they have faults? Yes! But continue to reach out with a hand to encourage and love. In this you will continue to bring great pleasure to My heart, and I will bestow great blessing upon your life.

You Have Done Well,

Your Loving Father

Loving Father,

Today, Father, I will continue reaching out a hand to encourage and love by:

Your Words of encouragement and love mean so much to me. They make all the struggles, trials, and stretching worthwhile. Thank You, Father, for helping me to be released from others' expectations of me, focusing instead on Your expectations of me. Most of all, thank You for making me a part of Your Master Plan.

Amen

"Beloved, if God loved us so [very much],
we also ought to love one another."
1 John 4:11 AMP

Day 138

My Child,

Allow My light to shine in your life, illuminating places of deception and uneasiness. Stand strong in your faith in Me. Be lifted up this day to know that My angels are round about you, and you will not strike your foot against a stone. Be not afraid. I have made your heart to be an open door to Me. Walk confidently in Me.

Continue On With Courage,

Your Father

Father,

What comfort to know that You protect me and have Your angels round about me, so that I can walk confidently in Your grace and love. Father, thank You that day by day, You continue to enrich and bless my life that my heart can fly freely with You.

Father, Show me any areas where I still walk in fear or distrust.

Amen

"Then you will walk in your way securely,
and in confident trust, and you shall not
dash your foot or stumble."
Proverbs 3:23 AMP

My Child,

I challenge you this day, to not let grievances get in the way. Establish this in your heart from the start; and refuse to receive darts thrown your way from the enemy, who hates to see you whole. Discharge them as they come your way. Remembrances of love extended are the establishing elements of life found in Me. Set all other memories free. Memories not found in love pollute the streams of living water flowing from a life consecrated in Me. Allow your heart to continue as an open door of My love to others, without fear. Reach out unafraid to hear, with eyes wide open, and discernment clear, continue to love. My protection over you is secure.

I Love You, My Child,

Your Father

Dearest Father,

You have taught me from the very beginning that love, acceptance, and forgiveness are Your way, and that every time a negative thought comes, I am to release it immediately into Your loving hands and replace it with joyous memory of Your faithfulness. Father, thank You for alerting me when I begin to allow thoughts to form that are not found in love.

Father, Is there any unforgiveness or grievances that I have let penetrate my heart and take up residence?

Amen

*"May Christ through your faith [actually] dwell
(settle down, abide, make His permanent home)
in your hearts! May you be rooted deep
in love and founded securely on love…."*
Ephesians 3:17 AMP

My Child,

Receive My blessings and the abundance of My heart. Simply release unto Me your cares and let Me disperse them as clouds on a summer day. Let Me reveal to you their source so that you do not take them into your heart. Be free this day, knowing that My hand is guiding you with My peace from above. Be carefree this day to soar and glide, and enjoy your life, abiding in Me. Seize each moment with optimism. Release My joy within your heart. Allow Me to place within you this day a sense of security that cannot be daunted. Listen to the quietness—in the quietness is My heart. Be established this day in the comfort of My love.

I Love You, My Child,

Your Father

Dear Father,

You bring such comfort and a sense of security to my heart. When I begin to struggle, thank You for reminding me to quiet my heart in Your Presence, knowing that peace will once again descend. Thank You, Father, for bringing such goodness into my life.

Father, Thank You for these blessings in my life:

Amen

"For You, Lord, will bless the [uncompromising] righteous [him who is upright and in right standing with You], as with a shield You will surround him with goodwill [pleasure and favor]."
Psalm 5:12 AMP

Day 141

My Child,

Into My Presence you have come. As you have lifted your heart in praise to Me, I've opened your heart that you might see My favor in everything you do, because I love you! Continue in this way, My child. Continue with a heart full of hope each day. Sit awhile within My Presence that you might continue to hear My plans and purposes for your life and that a newfound hope would burst forth in your daily walk. You will always find there is room for you in My Presence. Be encouraged and walk in this special way of blessing and fulfillment, all of your days.

You Are Precious To Me,

Your Loving Father

My Precious Father,

Precious Father, My hope is in You for:

The hope of my heart is fullfilled in spending time with You. You lavish me with favor and unconditional love, and my heart is filled with new courage. Your Words to my heart are so precious to me. Your love is my greatest treasure!

Amen

"My hope and expectation are in You."
Psalm 39:7 AMP

My Child,

It is My great pleasure to fill your life with peace. I am working within your heart, a new sense of calm and completeness. Enjoy the journey and receive My blessings awaiting you. Be at peace and enjoy the view. Let Me permeate your being with serenity and magnificence. Let go of the frenzied activity of each day. Peace, peace, marvelous peace, coming down from the Father above. Enfold it to your heart as a friend. There will always be time enough for activity. This is your time of peace. Relish it, My child.

Stay In My Peace,

Your Loving Father

My Loving Father,

When I stay in Your peace, there is such a sense of completeness. Thank You for intensifying Your peace and completeness in my life. When I begin to feel pressured and overwhelmed, help me come into Your Presence. Speak peace to my heart. Sometimes I feel that all I have to bring into my time with You are the dregs of my day, and yet You always receive me in—teaching me that You are always there for me!

Father, Thank You for Your unconditional Presence in my life.

Amen

"May mercy, [soul] peace, and love be multiplied to you."
Jude 2 AMP

My Child,

Let your life be a bright light. Let your life shine brilliantly that all may see its radiance and warming glow, for My glory is in you. Let it shine forth unhindered by the daily circumstances beyond your control. Let My Spirit of light and truth govern you, not the situations that would distract you. Walk with determination and choose to bless and bring forth the best in others with graciousness. All of Heaven proclaims My glory, and this glory will bless others as you allow My peace, love, and contentment to flow through you.

You Are Blessed,

Your Loving Father

Loving Father,

Father, Give me the words — Your Words — to speak today…that I would be able to bless those around me.

Thank You, Father, for teaching me day-by-day, to walk in Your power, and not to be distracted by the challenging events of the day. Help me to speak positive words of trust and faith in those moments to bring forth Your blessings, the best in me, and the best in others.

Amen

*"Shine (be radiant with the glory of the Lord),
for your light has come, and the glory
of the Lord has risen upon you!"
Isaiah 60:1 AMP*

My Child,

Don't struggle with the events of your life. Let Me filter them and make of them a masterpiece in your life. Release to Me control over each day. Walk in My peace. I will bring order and understanding and eliminate the unnecessary. You can depend on that. Now go forward with a light heart, depending on My love to bring you through to victory. Don't allow distractions to detain you along the way. Resist and then receive My best for you. I love you, My child. Let that truth resound in your heart, and you will always prevail!

Struggle Not, My Child!

Your Loving Father

Father,

As I've gone through the hardest times of my life, You have been there for me—an anchor of hope. Your protection and love have made me stronger and wiser. Thank You, Father, for guiding my life and protecting my way.

Father, Today I will rest and trust in Your protection.

Amen

"The Lord will give unyielding and impenetrable strength, to His people; the Lord will Bless His people with peace."
Psalm 29:11 AMP

Day 145

My Child,

Do you not know that I love you? It is My greatest desire to bless you. I want you to know Me with intimacy and love. I desire to spend time with you. Lay down your troubles and allow Me to touch your life with peace brought forth by relinquishment. Music sings in the life that is relinquished. It sings with abandon. Tremendous things lie ahead for you. Relinquishment shall bring it forth.

I Love You,

Your Father

Dear Father,

Father, I do love You and want to please You with my life.

I willingly relinquish my life to You, because I can trust You and I know You love me. You have always been my faithful and intimate friend. My life belongs to You! You are such an anchor in my life. I love You!

Amen

"O, love the Lord, all you His saints!
For the Lord preserves the faithful"
Psalm 31:23 AMP

My Child,

Set your eyes on Me and follow My every move by listening closely and maintaining a watchful eye. My protection is with you on the road ahead, and peace shall abound as you rest in My love. Gratitude and a thankful heart will give you wings to fly. Soar, My child, with eagle's wings and rejoice in My loving kindness. Don't strain to see ahead, for I see all and it is good. Relax. I have sustained you thus far. I shall continue to fashion and create beauty in your life and build your destiny with purpose and meaning. Trust Me to continue to bless you, lead, and guide you—to open and close doors of My choosing. You are blessed, My child.

Be At Rest In My Embrace,

Your Loving Father

Father,

So often I'm tempted to strain and try to see ahead, but when I relax in Your arms, stop struggling, and keep my eyes on You, I sense Your hand at work in my life. I do want to soar as an eagle, triumphantly in my life. Soaring with eagle's wings gives freedom and vision, Your vision. Thank You for leading and guiding every detail of my life with purpose. I am so blessed and grateful to You, Father.

Father, I am listening closely for Your direction.

Amen

"My whole being follows hard after You and clings closely to You; Your right hand upholds me."
Psalm 63:8 AMP

My Child,

Reflect back and you will see My Presence in every circumstance of your life. See, I have been watching over your life to bring you to a place of blessing and abundance. I have brought you thus far, and as you stretch out your wings to fly once more, I will reach out to you and with my hand undergird and guide you to a place of peace, serenity, and faith to complete the transition. Blessed is he who comes in the Name of the Lord. He is My delight. Come into My Presence with joy and abandon. Come unto Me without a care, no holding back—receive My refreshing life and the blessings I hold for you. Now go forth unafraid, knowing I, your Father, care for you.

You Are Blessed,

Your Loving Father

Father,

Father, I hand these matters over to You in absolute trust:

When I reflect back and see You in every circumstance of my life, it brings such joy to my heart. Things that seemed unexplainable before, suddenly take on new meaning and purpose. Transition is not always easy, but You have always been with me every step of the way. When I find myself becoming deflated and holding back, I will simply reflect back on the many ways You daily bless and care for me.

Amen

"And have clothed yourselves with the new [spiritual self], which is [ever in the process of being] renewed and remolded into [fuller and more perfect knowledge upon] knowledge after the image (the likeness) of Him Who created us."
Colossians 3:10 AMP

My Child,

I have preordained your way. I have created a life for you, full of purpose. It is My desire that you live victoriously. Little have you known of the strategic plans backing you up. Little have you seen of the preparations and intricate details arranged and executed on your behalf. And even now as you go forth in life you are preserved by My hand. Go forth unafraid, fully prepared to walk out your life with confidence and significance.

I Am With You,

Your Faithful Father

Thank You, Father,

Remind me that You are with me every step of the way, that I can trust You to take care of every detail in my life. Today, instead of getting caught up in the worries of life, I will turn my thoughts to You, with thanksgiving and love, ever listening for Your voice to my heart. I love You, Father!

Faithful Father, I will walk in absolute trust today.

Amen

"Eye has not seen, nor ear heard,
Nor have entered into the heart of man
The things which God has prepared
for those who love Him."
1 Corinthians 2:9 NKJV

My Child,

I have raised you up to be strong, resilient, and quietly assured of My care over you. I shall strengthen your resolve. I shall create you to be valiant and able to stand against frustration and resentment. Strings from the past will no longer tie you down or incapacitate you. Cares and worries fade away as you continue to rest in My love.

You Are Strong In Me,

Your Loving Father

Dear Father,

Father, Are there areas in my life, that I'm not aware of, where I need to walk in acceptance and forgiveness?

Help me to be strong. My greatest goal in life is to love as You love. Loving with Your love, nothing is impossible! With Your love, frustration and resentment from the past fade away. Father, I lay down the negatives of my life and choose instead to love with Your love, with acceptance and forgiveness.

Amen

"Who were chosen and foreknown by God the Father and consecrated (sanctified, made holy) by the Spirit to be obedient to Jesus Christ (the Messiah)"
1 Peter 1:2 AMP

My Beloved Child,

Listen with your whole heart. Resist the temptation to lean on your own understanding. Release unto Me the weight of the world upon your shoulders. Release the responsibilities, misunderstandings, inequities, longings, confusions, wranglings, casualties, seeming inabilities, conflicts, and mistakes, and give them to Me. Sit in My Presence and listen to My heart, with a knowing that My peace shall continue to rest upon your life.

I Am With You,

Your Loving Father

Father,

Help me to continue to release unto You every care, fault, and area where I have come up short. Thank You, Father, for helping me every step of every day. And Father, thank You for the freedom I feel right now with that weight gone!

Dear Father, I want to praise and thank You with great joy for Your faithfulness and care over my life.

Amen

"Speak, Lord, for Your servant is listening."
1 Samuel 3:9 AMP

My Child,

It is My desire that you grow and be transformed. I have brought you through much change. It has challenged and stretched you and caused you to grow. Change is the door through which you find out what you are really made of. Change brings discovery and expands your vision. Your life will continue to transform, expand, broaden, and be refined by My truth and love. Don't fear the future. It is held securely by My hand of love. I have led you thus far and will not abandon you but will instead guide you toward My perfect design for your life.

I Will Not Fail You,

Your Loving Father

Faithful Father,

When I am tempted to worry, help me remember the many times You have touched my life and shown me a better way. Even when I feel challenged and stretched, I trust You, Father, to secure Your way for my life and bring me safely through.

Father, Thank You for teaching me to look to You for the answers.

Amen

"Do not be conformed to this world (this age),
[fashioned after and adapted to its external,
superficial customs], but be transformed
(changed) by the [entire] renewal of your mind…"
Romans 12:2 AMP

My Child,

Stand resolute and confident in Me. Continue on learning straightforwardness, patience, peace in the midst of the storm, forgiveness, faithfulness, perseverance, and diplomacy that you might come forth even stronger. Determination has served you well. Look to Me for guidance. It is My pleasure to bless you as you continue to seek Me and flourish. Discover the fruit of your labors and it will taste sweet.

You Have Done Well, My Child,

Your Loving Father

Dear Father,

Knowing You are pleased with me fills my heart with joy! Thank You that in the uncertainties, You have always been there, encouraging and cheering me on, through little and big ways, letting me know that I am exactly where You want me to be. You are so faithful!

Loving Father, I want to spend time with You today in Your loving Presence!

Amen

"Off in just and right sacrifices; trust
(lean on and be confident) in the Lord."
Psalm 4:4 AMP

My Child,

Stand fast, My child, unwavering, solid on the foundation of My Word. My faithfulness has and shall continue to sustain you through the tough times, and the blessings of My heart shall continue to delight you and bring you joy. Fortitude will become a way of life for you, sustained by an inner peace, brought forth by time spent with Me. Continue investing your time with Me, and discover the abundant blessings I have awaiting you.

I Love You,

Your Father

Loving Father,

Father, What is on Your heart for me today?

You truly have been faithful throughout my life, holding me steady through every storm, teaching me Your truths day by day, loving and protecting me and showing me Your ways. Gratitude and thankfulness overwhelm my heart with joy. I love You, Father!

Amen

"Guide me in Your truth and faithfulness and teach me, for You are the God of my salvation: for You [You only and altogether] do I wait [expectantly] all the day long."
Psalm 25:5 AMP

Day 154

My Child,

Trace your footsteps in life and see that there has been a pattern, a direction and a plan. Stand fast, My child, for I will never forsake you. Rejoice and be glad, for I have a preordained plan and direction for your life. Nothing is too hard for Me. I will bring light in the darkness and prepare a way through the hard times. Be a shining example to those around you, and share My love and compassion with others. And you will find that magnificent and beyond comprehension are My ways.

You Are Complete In Me,

Your Loving Father

You are awesome, God!

Through the most difficult of times, You have been there with me, encouraging and leading the way. When the journey seems hard, You infuse hope and even joy in the most unexpected places. How can I not love You, Father. You mean everything to me!

Loving Father, Who can I share Your hope and love with today?

Amen

"How beautiful are the feet of those who bring glad tidings! (How welcome is the coming of those who preach the Good News of His good things!)"
Romans 10:15 AMP

Day 155

My Child,

Begin each day straight forward, unhindered by the past. Complete the job set before you with honor and praise. My light will shine before you, leading, guiding, and illuminating the dark corners you encounter. Rejoice, for a new day shines brightly before you. Carry not the hindrances of the past into the present. Leave them in the past and move on to better, more fruitful days. Sail on, My child! Sail on!

You Are Blessed, My Child,

Your Loving Father

Dear Father,

Loving Father, Please show me any residue from the past that I may still be holding on to.

What freedom it brings to be able to live for the pure joy of living, free from negatives of the past or expectations for the future. Thank You, Father, for helping me to release the past, day-by-day, safely into Your arms of love.

Amen

"You have proved my heart; You have visited me in the night; You have tried me and find nothing [no evil purpose in me]; I have purposed that my mouth shall not transgress."
Psalm 17:3 AMP

My Child,

Sing forth and proclaim the Word of the Lord. Let it ring in your heart, and the blessings of God will arise in your life. There will be no doubt as to Who is your Lord and to Whom you owe your allegiance, for the truth of your heart will shine forth from your countenance. Don't fear the future, for it is in My hands and secure from all uncertainty. My truth will reign in your life. So be at peace and let the burdens roll off like the dead weights that they are. Establish your heart upon absolute trust in Me.

Be Free, My Child, Be Free!

Your Father

Loving Father,

I choose to rejoice in the now, to be at peace, and to give the burdens of my life over to You. I choose to be free! When my mind begins to struggle, I will purpose to delight in today and be released from unnecessary battles of the mind. Thank You, Father, for my freedom in You!

Father, Today I choose to give You my burdens of:

Amen

"For I will proclaim the name [and Presence] of the Lord. Concede and ascribe greatness to our God."
Deuteronomy 32:3 AMP

My Child,

Circumstances are moments in time. Don't allow them to control whole segments of your thought life. Give others grace, as I have given you grace. Leave yesterday behind, and live today unhindered and unencumbered by tomorrow. Be merciful and forgiving of others in your life. Leave the past behind, and live totally in the present, rejoicing in the blessings and benefits therein. Cancel old debts and mark them paid!

Love As I Love,

Your Father

My Father,

Father, Are there old debts that I have held on to that I need to cancel and mark paid?

Help me to always remember to leave yesterday behind, and to live today. Show me how to walk in forgiveness towards others. It is my desire to live today totally in Your Presence, in Your peace, receiving and giving Your love, giving and receiving Your grace.

Amen

"For if you forgive men their trespasses,
your Heavenly Father will also forgive you."
Matthew 6:14 NKJV

My Child,

You may be asking yourself, "Which direction should I go?" Don't allow yourself to be caught up in confusion. Listen to the Words spoken by My Spirit. Heed these Words of strength and direction. Stand and be faithful to the commands of your Lord and Savior. Mark these Words in your heart, and then remain resolute with determination to finish the course with distinction. Stand strong and absolute on My Words.

I Am Directing Your Paths,

Your Loving Father

Father,

You have taught me that where Your peace is, there Your Spirit is also. When my life seems uncertain, plant in my heart the seeds of hope and abundant life. At those times help me to simply be at peace and know that You have cleared the way before me, that one step at a time is sufficient, as I press forward toward the mark.

Father, I bring this area of my life to You for direction and peace:

Amen

"In all your ways know, recognize and acknowledged Him, and He will direct and make straight and plain your paths."
Proverbs 3:6 AMP

My Child,

Be not afraid of the long journey ahead. The course brings with it added distinction and fulfillment of dreams. Renew your spirit. Take on new provisions for the trip and set sail once more, with new determination to finish the voyage to the end with faithfulness. Set your heart toward the sweet victory of success. There is time enough for understanding and fulfillment. Now is the time for determined resilience brought forth by praise and an upright heart. Ride, freely glide, upon this free-flowing voyage of life. Progress flows easily within the confines of My love. Pass under bridges; drift through open country. Then as darkness falls, continue to float unrestricted and unafraid, for I am there. I am your guide. Be not affected by the fears of fellow travelers. Rest in Me. Be at peace and enjoy the passage.

Together Forever,

Your Loving Father

Faithful Father,

Father, What are the "new provisions" You need for me to take on for my journey in life?

There is such beauty and safety navigating through life with You. Thank You, Father, for giving me ears to hear Your plans for my life. Help calm my fears with the knowledge of Your faithfulness and love.

Amen

"I have chosen the way of truth and faithfulness;
Your ordinances have I set before me."
Psalm 119:30 AMP

My Child,

A covenant I make with you this day. You have searched long and hard and have found Me. You have made of your heart a resting place for My peace and joy. Now, I say to you, "I shall go before you to bring you into new realms of My glory, righteousness, and right standing with Me." You have remained faithful. Now, I shall lengthen your days and bring forth abundance to your spirit—overflowing to bring forth My will in your life. Gaze ahead to My glory. Seek to walk closer with Me. The doors shall open with astounding precision, and you shall walk through them jubilantly. Get ready. We shall walk through together, unrestrained. My Spirit shall draw forth from you all that I have promised, for My heart of love has deposited it within you for this day. So rejoice and know the fulfillment from My heart of love.

My Precious Child,

Your Loving Father

Loving Father,

My heart sings for the joy of Your companionship and love. It is so wonderful to see my life changed with the realization that You created me to be in covenant and relationship with You. There is no safer or more blessed place on earth to be. Thank You for Your promises and Your precious love!

Gracious Father, I want to pour out my love to You today.

Amen

"The secret [of the sweet satisfying companionship]
of the Lord have they who fear (revere and worship)
Him, and He will show them His covenant and
reveal to them its [deep, inner] meaning."
Psalm 25:14 AMP

Day 161

My Child,

Victory comes through speaking forth the truth of My Words in love. When one speaks through compassion, it brings life. Display kindness. Become long-suffering. Administer an abundance of grace. Be as My ministering angels who bring forth peace and warmth, and hope where indifference has settled, offer compassion.

Love As I Love,

Your Loving Father

Precious Father,

Father, Today this is how I want to pour out my love to You:

Many times You have said that one of the great purposes of our lives here on earth is to learn to love as You love, to be a living testament of Your mercy. Father, all things are possible through You when the desires of our hearts are the desires of Your heart. Father, I am willing to love with Your love.

Amen

"Love endures long and is patient and kind;"
1 Corinthians 13:4 AMP

My Child,

Strength, love, and compassion come forth unabated when one rests in the comfort of My hand. Be assured, My child, that your perils, worries, and concerns shall fall away as you trust in the liberty of My love. The goal is freedom of understanding and acceptance of the fullness of My love in your life. Seek Me, and receive rejuvenation daily. Shake off the burdens, restraints, and offenses of today. They are not yours to bear.

Rest In My Love,

Your Father

Loving Father,

Thank You for daily helping me to achieve the ultimate goal of understanding and accepting the fullness of Your love in my life. Now I am free to love others unconditionally, with no strings attached. Thank You, Father, for the magnitude of Your love!

Father, Today I want to give You my worries and concerns, and rest in the comfort of Your loving hand.

Amen

"Whereas the object and purpose of our instruction and charge is love, which springs from a pure heart and a good [clear] conscience and sincere [unfeigned] faith."

1 Timothy 1:5 AMP

My Precious One,

This freedom of heart and soul that is yours to enjoy comes in stages. You will understand its progression so that others can follow the same trail with understanding. You have followed the path I have laid before you, holding tightly to My hand with trust in the finished outcome. My heart rejoices with you, for your heart knows full well the joys of trusting and walking with your Father, your friend. Be blessed this day, dear child of Mine!

Your Loving Father

Loving Father,

Precious Father, My heart reaches out to You with such joy and gratefulness!

Holding tightly to Your hand with the trust of a child has been the joy of my life! Help me to remain on the paths You have set before me, always trusting in You. Let me not forget that You are not only my loving Father, but also my friend.

Amen

"That He may teach us His ways and that we may walk in His paths."
Isaiah 2:3 AMP

Day 164

My Child,

Grace is a state of freedom, liberty to be unencumbered by what you see and hear. What does My truth say? My grace is sufficient! What does My love say? You are complete in Me! Ride the winds of adversity with confidence and let Me bear the burdens. Rejoice, for victory is walking in the freedom of My love.

Be Free In Me!

Your Loving Father

Loving Father,

More and more You are training me to be at peace and trust You. The hardest lesson is letting You carry my cares. I don't realize that I am carrying them until I get so weary from the weight. Thank You, Father, for reminding me to give my burdens to You.

Father, What burdens am I carrying now, that I need to turn over to You?

Amen

"Every good gift and every perfect (free, large, full) gift is from above; it comes down from the Father of all"
James 1:17 AMP

When God Speaks to My Heart

Day 165

My Child,

My ways bring life. Throughout history, those who have learned to serve Me well have discovered absolute contentment. Through relationship with Me they have found happiness and freedom from the daily concerns of life. Spend time with Me. Keep your focus on Me and witness profound changes in your life as you move into a covering of blessing.

You Are Loved,

Your Father

Dear Father,

Father, Today I will seek to spend more time with You.

Help me, I pray, to more faithfully come to You for wisdom in managing my time. Remind me to stop and spend moments alone with You. Help me to hear Your Words of encouragement and love.

Amen

*Your kingdom come, Your will be done
on earth as it is in heaven."
Matthew 6:10 AMP*

Day 166

My Child,

I am your deliverer and your protector. Learn to abide under the shadow of My wing and listen for My voice. Give Me your concerns and trust in My watchful, protecting power. Serve Me with your whole heart and walk proudly in who you are as My child. Walk steadfast and with undaunted trust. Does My Word not say that I will deliver you from every trial—every struggle? Step forth proudly in the service of your King, and together we shall see victory after victory!

You Are Blessed,

Your Father

Loving Father,

When life is hard, teach me to look to You for guidance and direction. In every season and every struggle, show me how to place my faith and confidence in You. Bring a knowing into my heart that You are always near. Remind me to follow Your voice when I am distracted so I can walk satisfied and rejoicing in life.

Faithful Father, Teach me absolute trust in You.

Amen

"When the righteous cry for help, the Lord hears, and delivers them out of all their distress and troubles."
Psalm 34:17 AMP

My Child,

Remain steadfast in your walk with Me. Rely upon My faithfulness—a faithfulness that never fails. It brings forth the fruit sown. Be constant to seek My Presence in your life, and see My Words come to life and bless you. Continue on, undaunted, by the passing scene. My promises shall come forth at the appointed time. Seek only to be immersed in My vast sea of love and My Presence.

Seek To Know Me!

Your Faithful Father

My Father,

Loving Father, I long to know You more!

Each day is a priceless gift from You, even when hope seems deferred and the way seems hard. Help me remember that every day carries the mark of Your love. Bless my life with the fruit of the good seed I've sown. Touch my life with goodness, mercy, and hope.

Amen

"But if from there you will seek [inquire for and require as necessity] the Lord your God, you will find Him if you [truly] seek Him with all your heart [and mind] and soul and life."
Deuteronomy 4:29 AMP

Day 168

My Child,

Be a pliable twig in My hands, and I shall mold you into an arrow—always finding your mark. Relax in My Presence and be confident in My love as a refuge for you. Difficulties will come and go, but My protection shall sustain you in all areas of your life. Draw peace from above. Seek happiness and make melody in your heart. Seek each new day as a brand-new start. Nothing will be able to pull you apart from My absolute authority and stability in your life. Refuse doubt. Believe My Word! Focus your mind and heart on Me!

Be Confident In Me,

Your Loving Father

Loving Father,

As I walk step-by-step, holding Your hand, I will trust You, undaunted and unafraid. This is how I choose to live, so that You can mold me into an arrow, always finding my mark! I love You, Father!

Father, What areas of my life do I need to become more pliable?

Amen

"But without faith it is impossible to please Him, for he who comes to God must believe that He is, and that He is a rewarder of those who diligently seek Him."
Hebrews 11:6 NKJV

My Child,

Live your life with confidence and a willingness to accept others where they are. Extend your hand in fellowship, not holding accounts of wrongs or slights. My Spirit within you desires to reach out with love. Slights will fade away and peace and calm shall return. Reach out! Reach out to that one in need and say, "My Lord will provide for you. He has not forsaken you nor abandoned you in your hour of need," for My angels shall watch over that one in need and bring him through to the other side. Many are the trials of this life, but My love transcends all trials. Let them know of My love for them! Let them know!

Love As I Love,

Your Father

Dearest Father,

Loving Father, Who can I bless today with Your encouraging Words?

Help me to experience the joy of speaking Your words in love and encouragement to others. I want to be able to impart Your compassion, into the crevices of each aching heart and find that those words have been anointed by Your Spirit. Give me the words to share that will make a difference and bless those around me.

Amen

"We are telling you about what we ourselves have actually seen and heard, so that you may share the fellowship and the joys we have with the Father and with Jesus Christ His Son."
1 John 1:3 TLB

My Child,

Challenges will come in life, but hold fast to My hand. Don't walk in fear, but be carefree and rejoice in the God of your salvation. You shall be safe and secure as you seek My face continually and speak forth My promises to you. Surefooted strength is My gift to you. Faith and circumstances work together to create whole and satisfied life for those who place absolute trust in Me. The truth of My Word shall ring forth and bring triumph and freedom. Look to My Word and trust in My love to conquer every challenge holding you back.

You Are Protected By My Love,

Your Father

Father,

I stand convinced of Your power to change, mold, and shape my life. Help me to continue to look to You when life becomes challenging. Day-by-day, Father, as I see Your promises in my life fulfilled—I am so grateful!

Loving Father, how would You have me grow today?

Amen

"Be assured and understand that the trial and proving of your faith bring out endurance and steadfastness and patience."
James 1:3 AMP

My Precious Child,

Stand back and watch Me work. Watch the canvas take shape and form with color and vibrancy. The shades of the palette are coming together to make a beautiful picture for others to gaze upon and see the beauty of God. Cultivate vision by looking to Me and implementing your life into the big picture. Vision brings structure, and structure brings strength. See, and in seeing, believe!

See As I See!

Your Father

Loving Father,

Faithful Father, Your love overwhelms me with joy.

Create a masterpiece of beauty in me. Thank You for the many beautiful and vibrant colors in my life, proclaiming a statement of Your faithfulness and love. I know You will complete what You have begun in me with perfection. I am overwhelmed with delight and joy because of the gifts You have given as a doting Father to me.

Amen

"Where there is no vision [no redemptive revelation of God], the people perish."
Proverbs 29:18 AMP

I Love You, My Child,

It shall become clear to you the path that you shall take. The way will be bathed in light so that you shall not miss it, be distracted, or get sidetracked. The vision will become strong and remain. Don't worry or be distraught, but know that what I have planned for you shall be, and you shall rejoice and be glad. Carry on with a song in your heart and determination to finish the way with honor. My blessings go with you, My child. The refreshing of mind, body, soul, and spirit shall come to build you up. Press onward! Press onward!

There Is Much To Learn!

Your Loving Father

Loving Father,

When I think I cannot take another step, You overwhelm me with Your Presence and Your joy. Suddenly I have the strength to go on. When I become discouraged and weary, You send someone to reach out to me with encouragement and love. You take such good care of me, Father!

Faithful Father, Speak to my heart, for I am listening!

Amen

"All the paths of the Lord are mercy and steadfast love,
even truth and faithfulness are they for those
who keep His covenant, and His testimonies."
Psalm 25:10 AMP

Day 173

My Child,

Many times, I have said unto you, "Let not your heart be troubled." Listen once again to the strains of My Words, "Let not your heart be troubled." Let your heart rest within the confines of My love, listening not to the enemy, but hearing and seeing My Word and relying on My truth. Contend not with conflicting reports, but stand firm in My love, and let Me make the moves—be content to watch and wait. Resist not the tides as they ebb and flow, but know that the ebb and flow shall form boundaries of beauty. Stand in My love. Release it all unto Me and rejoice.

Let Not Your Heart Be Troubled!

Your Father

Precious Father,

Dear Father, Thank You for filling my heart with Your peace.

Help me to see things as You do. To register all You bring my way, and weigh it in the balance of Your love. To always respond within the guidelines of Your Word to me. To be refreshed, and respond, with the freshness of Your Holy Spirit. Help me remember that standing on Your Word—the results are sure!

Amen

"Let not your heart be troubled, neither let it be afraid."
John 14:27 NKJV

My Child,

I will lead you into experiences that will have no road map. Learn to enjoy the beauty of unexplored territory. You will need My guidance for each step. Others shall follow to make it a well marked trail, deeply imprinted across the wilderness. You shall be among this new breed of trailblazers, but a trailblazer must be disciplined. Accept the mantle of obedience. Surefootedness is brought about through sustained patience. Persevere and we shall see it through to the very end.

I Am With You, My Child!

Your Loving Father

Precious Father,

After all these years, I still find myself seeking the security of a road map, by looking to others to bring me comfort and guidance, instead of You! Forgive me, Father! Thank You for Your sustained faith in me. Show me how to follow You with my whole heart.

Dear Father, I come to You today for guidance and wisdom.

Amen

"And the Lord shall guide you continually..."
Isaiah 58:11 AMP

My Child,

Seek, and you shall find. Knock, and the door shall be opened to you. Abide under the shadow of My wing. Patience has caused My Spirit to flourish within you. The tether has been cut and you shall begin to rise to be carried along by My Spirit. I have charted a course by which you shall travel. The scenery shall be breathtakingly beautiful, and you shall partake of the miraculous along the way. Maintain your balance with constant prayer. See, it shall become a way of life, and together we shall see the pieces of the horizon come together as a beautiful picture.

You Are Blessed, My Child!

Your Loving Father

Loving Father,

Dear Father, How would You have me pray today?

Even with all the ups and downs of each day, walking with You, there is such beauty within each day! Father, when I forget to pray and instead put my focus on the passing scene, draw me back, that prayer might truly be a way of life for me! Thank You, Father!

Amen

"He who dwells in the secret place of the Most High
Shall abide under the shadow of the Almighty."
Psalm 91:1 NKJV

My Precious One,

Rise up, My child! Come fly with Me! Release your heart from all that would tie you down and come soar with Me! Proclaim My goodness and My love to the world! Upon the canvas of your heart, I proclaim a brand-new start, free and unencumbered, for it's My heart of love that guides you. Go forth today, confident in every way, that I, your Lord and King, have answers for everything. Your way is secure as we proceed, hand in hand.

Sing And Be Free!

Your Loving Father

Precious Father,

You have been so good to me. Thank You for lovingly reminding me to release my heart once again from all that would tie it down, to walk in freedom with You.

Father, Today I will speak of Your goodness in my life.

Amen

"I will proclaim the name of the LORD;
how glorious is our God!"
Deuteronomy 32:3 NLT

Dear Child Of My Heart,

My peace is beginning to descend as never before because you are learning that it is not about you, but about My ability to come through and bless you in all that you do. You are learning to be free from all that pulls and drags down. Be confident, be secure. It's not a time to just endure. It is a time to grow, thrive, and really feel alive in My Presence. Enjoy every moment of every day as you learn to live this life in abundance.

You Are Loved,

Your Father

Dear Father,

Precious Father, Speak to my heart today, as I work, sing, laugh, and play!

How wonderful to know that it's important to You that we not only love You and one another, but that we also know how to have fun together. I am often so intent on living life with purpose, that I forget to "play." Thank You, Father, for once again teaching me, and my friends, how to have fun and pleasure in life. The most wonderful part is that You are right there with us, enjoying it is much as we are and cheering us on.

Amen

*"O LORD my God, in You, I take refuge
and put my trust."*
Psalm 7:1 AMP

Day 178

My Precious Child,

There is a freshness in your life that has come in on the breezes of My love. It is a newness that shall remain. Restored, refreshed, renewed. This is My promise to you. Enjoy its ever present blessing for you. It brings with it a childlike freedom and grace as never before. Enjoy the laughter and fun that come with it. Let your heart and mind be renewed in Me.

Relish The Freedom Of This Day!

Your Loving Father

Precious Father,

Your Word says, "The joy of the Lord is our strength!" For truly laughter brings strength and renewal. Father, help me remember to have fun in life, even when circumstances would appear just the opposite. I love You so much!

Father, Show me how to cast my cares today.

Amen

*"And be constantly renewed in the spirit of your mind
[having a fresh mental and spiritual attitude],"*
Ephesians 4:23 AMP

My Child,

Flourish and bloom. Take each day as it comes, with an open heart. Each day is a gift to you from My heart. Patience has led the way as each day you have come to me for direction and leading. You have delighted in the simple pleasure of life, as each test and trial has brought you closer to the safety of My heart. Walk in the realm of peace every day by releasing the turmoil to Me and letting peace descend, counting on Me to bring the answers. Silence the spirit of anxiety with My spirit of peace and joy. Proceed this day with a light heart, My child.

I Love You,

Your Father

Dear Father,

Loving Father, I want to make the very best of today.

You have, through Your love and grace, caused to me to flourish and bloom. You have loved and protected me. Thank You, Father, for teaching me day-by-day to silence anxiety with Your spirit of peace and joy.

Amen

*"The wilderness, and the dry land shall be glad;
the desert shall rejoice and blossom like the rose..."*
Isaiah 35:1 AMP

My child,

It is just the beginning. The Heavens declare My glory, and so shall your life. Enjoy this time of rest and pleasure with Me. Be My friend, and the joy of that friendship will open the door to everything else. Draw to your heart My love and peace each day that life's static would be released, and you might hear clearly as you move forward, moment-by-moment. Go forth today with confidence.

I Take Pleasure In You, My Child,

Your Loving Father

Father,

The sound of Your voice fills the air with Your joy! Fill my home with Your glory. Pour forth that which is in Your heart— into mine. As I listen to Your voice each day and fill my home with Your glory, at the end of the day, I can truly say, "Mission Accomplished!"

Loving Father, I want to pour out my heart to You, with such joy and gladness.

Amen

"For the Lord takes pleasure in His people;"
Psalm 149:4 AMP

My Child,

Total joy comes at a price, the price of relinquishment—relinquishment of the past and all its sorrows and dreams unfulfilled. Let it all go and you will find new joy and peace of mind. Time and time again you've looked to Me to set you free. And now, My precious one, you'll find that you have been set free, complete with a new sensitivity and creativity.

You Are Free!

Your Loving Father

Father,

Thank You, dear Father, for helping me let go of the past.

Masterfully You have designed my life, to make the picture full and complete. Help me, Father, to make the right choices in life and to relinquish the past. Thank You, Father, for caring about every detail of my life!

Amen

*"…Your youth, renewed, is like the eagles
[strong, overcoming…soaring]!"*
Psalm 103:5 AMP

My Precious One,

You bring such pleasure to Me. It is My pleasure to bring you from hopelessness to hope. I want to bring you from mediocrity to destiny. From sadness to joy. From loneliness to love. From fear to faith. From distrust and isolation to trust. I want you to live in victory. Faithfulness, hope, trust, love, honor, joy, and faith are the victorious foundations I offer you. Rest and be at peace. Live life to its fullest, and be blessed in this time set aside for you, My precious bride!

I Love You!

Your Father

Dear Father,

I need Your help to take full advantage of these moments of renewal, to truly rest and not waste the time. I want to come out of this time refreshed, restored, and ready for anything, led by Your heart. Help me to always start each day with You.

Father, Thank You for this time of rest.

Amen

"…and as the bridegroom rejoiceth over the bride,
so shall thy God rejoice over thee."
Isaiah 62:5

My Child,

Stand still and know that I am God. I will be glorified in your life. Many times I have held you in My hands and close to My heart. That is where you are now. Rest and let Me restore you to begin anew. For now, let Me fill your heart with gladness. Let Me fill your heart with song. Let Me make your life worth living. It's a time to enjoy My peace and My Presence. It's a time to sing and dance. Release your cares and worries, and you shall truly know fulfillment at last. Relinquish all that has held you captive. Simply enjoy each day by My hand of blessing. Rest now and be at peace.

You Are Loved!

Your Father

Father,

Loving Father, Help me rest in Your love for me today.

Thank You for always being there for me. There is no place I'd rather be than held by Your hands and close to Your heart. I love You, Father!

Amen

"And my God will liberally supply [fill to
the full] your every need according to
His riches in glory in Christ Jesus."
Philippians 4:19 AMP

My Child,

Leave the hurts behind like old clothes. Size up the situation, forgive, and go on. Reach into My heart and grasp My kind of love. Earnestly remember, My love is your highest calling. Grasp the essence of it all, love given for its own sake, not for its return. To give that sort of love you must be secure in My love. Stand secure in My love and watch your life be transformed, for I am with you. My rod and My staff are guiding you, and you shall live in the House of the Lord, forevermore.

Love As I Love,

Your Father

Loving Father,

You have blessed my life beyond measure. I am secure in Your love. Thank You, Father, for Your faithful and all encompassing love!

Dear Father, I will take comfort in Your Presence today.

Amen

"Yea, though I walk through the valley of the shadow
of death, I will fear no evil; For You are with me;
Your rod and Your staff, they comfort me."
Psalm 23:4 NKJV

Day 185

My Child,

Stand clear, stand out of the way and watch My hand of blessing fall upon you. Watch it flow and bring refreshing, newness, and life. Restored you shall be, free to receive from Me all that you have believed for. Resist the temptation to reach ahead too soon. Let Me transform your life and establish your way. All shall be in order and solidly placed. Watch with anticipation and blessed assurance.

You Are Blessed!

Your Loving Father

Dear Father,

Father, Help renew my mind today that I might start this day with a fresh slate.

With You every moment of every day has purpose and meaning! What a journey it has been, and what a journey it is yet to be. Thank You, Father, that there is restoration, newness, life, refreshing, freedom, and blessings ahead! Help me to continue looking ahead each day, led by You, with anticipation and joy!

Amen

"Restore to me the joy of my salvation and uphold me with a willing spirit."
Psalm 51:12 AMP

My Child,

Be strong and stand firm in your faith and trust in Me. My foundation of truth has been established since before time began. Persevere with patience. Oppressive winds will blow, but I will see you through it all. My strong hands of love will hold you steady and provide the leadership needed for you to prevail and continue forward with your destiny. Strong and mighty winds have blown, but the outcome is sure. The strength you will obtain is immeasurable. Stand strong, My child.

Be Strong In Me, My Child!

Your Loving Father

Loving Father,

Help me to be patient and to stand strong when I am weary from the passing events of my life. Thank You for lining up the marginal areas in my life, burning away the dross, and making me strong! Through it all, You've held me steady and secure.

Wonderful Father, I will look to You today for my strength.

Amen

"Stand firm in the Lord, my beloved."
Philippians 4:1 AMP

My Precious One,

The depths of the soul are tilled by deeper fellowship with Me. To know Me one must stay in constant and meaningful fellowship with Me. Contained within the human heart is the ability to know and walk in a continuous, significant relationship with Me, but few do. Spiritual awareness is the key. It opens the door to communion, sweet communion, with your Maker and Friend. The door is wide open. Please enter in and talk with Me and discover new, refreshing vistas through precious fellowship with Me. The door is open. Walk through!

Know Me, My Child!

Your Father

Precious and Loving Father,

Loving Father, I'm walking through that door, to have a lifelong, meaningful relationship with You, starting now!

I do truly want to know You more! I want to walk and talk with You continually! Help me, I pray, to listen to Your heart each day, moment by moment, and to share my thoughts, emotions, hopes, and dreams, desires, disappointments, and victories with You! Thank You, Father, that the door is open! It is my desire to enter in.

Amen

"Yes, everything else is worthless when compared with the priceless gain of knowing Christ Jesus my Lord."
Philippians 3:8 NLT

My Child,

Sanctification is a painful struggle, but it brings forth fruit immeasurable. Let My peace reign in your heart this day. Let My serenity invade your soul and reveal the way to absolute contentment in life. Be enmeshed in My love and removed from the clamor and distractions of life. Strive to know more of Me. Persevere on your journey and know that I will be there by your side—every step of the way. The Heavens resound with joy at the strengthening of one who seeks. Go forth unencumbered by reservations. Raise your heart in praise.

My Love Will Carry You Through!

Your Loving Father!

Dearest Father,

In the hardest of circumstances, Your love has carried me through. How could I ever doubt You when You have been so faithful to me. Yet, it is a day-by-day decision to come into Your rest and peace. Father, I do want Your peace in my life so much that I am determined to walk in contentment— whatever it takes. Thank You, Father, that day-by-day, You strengthen my resolve!

Father, These are the areas that I have been anxious about and I turn them over to You, so that I can go forth unencumbered by doubt!

Amen

"Because he has set his love upon Me, therefore will I deliver him; I will set him on high, because he knowns and understands My name.... He shall call upon Me, and I will answer him: I will be with him in trouble; I will deliver him, and honor him."
Psalm 91:14-15 AMP

Dear One,

You have learned many lessons in life and have looked to Me in the hard and challenging times. You are My child in whom I am well pleased. Don't place your confidence in people, places, or things, but place your confidence in My ability to come forth in you and to handle all circumstances, to bring victory and My way for you. You've believed in the past. Believe it now. Take counsel, but bring it to Me before you act on it.

Trust In Me,

Your Faithful Father

Loving Father,

Father, Today I want to bring these issues to You for Your loving counsel and wisdom:

I place my love and trust in You. I will let my heart rest and be content, for You bring contentment, fulfillment, and completeness to my life. Thank You, Father, for Your blessed counsel and Your love!

Amen

"Yet the Lord is faithful, and He will strengthen
[you] and set you on a firm foundation
and guard you from the evil [one]."
2 Thessalonians 3:3 AMP

My Child,

Walk in the sound Word of righteousness. Impress it upon your heart by My Spirit. Be steadfast in the knowledge of My love and faithfulness. Keep your stance of faith. You are not tainted by the past, but free to move ahead unencumbered. Step forth into the future, free to move and live and have your being in the strength and purity of My love. Be secure in the knowledge of who I have created you to be. Now unto Him who has provided all that you need, be glory forever!

Walk In The Freedom Of My Love!

Your Father

Thank You, Father,

For letting me see day-by-day through Your eyes, who You have created me to be, and the purpose for which You have created me. Thank You for giving me a sense of my intended future and a strong desire to fulfill that destiny!

Father, Help me to see this day through Your eyes.

Amen

"For in Him we live and move and have our being;"
Acts 17:28 AMP

My Child,

Stake your claim by My Spirit. Seek Me daily through My Word and promises. Let it be your pillar of strength. My authority and Word are your strength. Stand on it. Let it saturate your being. Let it be the energy that moves you. My Word—your life and being! Rejoice in My Word. It is there to stay and causes you to grow in strength each day. Go forth in the strength of My Word!

I Love You,

Your Father

Precious Father,

Father, What would You have me meditate on from Your Word today?

Your Word truly is my life and very being! It brings me strength when I am weary. Your promises bring me hope. But most of all, having intimate communion with You is life! Thank You for always being there for me! I love You, Father!

Amen

*"The Lord is my Strength and Song;
and He has become my Salvation."*
Psalm 118:14 AMP

Day 192

My Child,

You have stood. You have prevailed. You have remained steady in the face of apparent destruction. But know this, My child, the tide of the enemy shall not prevail, for I have placed My anointing upon you and My cloak of righteousness around you. My angels protect you. See, My child, the night does become day and all that has brought pain shall be brushed away. The dawning of the new day shall bring healing to your heart. So, arise and be whole. The light of My countenance shall shine about you and bring you peace!

I Have Sustained You,

Your Loving Father

Dear Father,

You have said You would go before me in all matters. Help me to trust You and to not become despondent or impatient. I know Your timing is perfect and what You have begun in my life You will complete. You have proved Yourself so faithful in my life! Thank You, Father, for bringing healing to every area of my life!

Father, What areas of my life am I not aware of that need healing?

Amen

"O Lord my God, I cried to You and You have healed me."
Psalm 30:2 AMP

When God Speaks to My Heart

My Child,

The steps of a righteous man are ordered by the Lord, that his life might shine forth the radiance of God. Light and darkness are alike to Me. I work in both and bring forth My attributes in the midst of trials and in the sunniest of days. Fear not the times of challenge, but stand strong in My Presence, redeeming the time with anticipation, drawn forth from hope in Me. You shall see results, for I have placed within you patience and hope which shall not be blotted out. Remain in My love and prevail.

I Am Always With You,

Your Loving Father

Loving Father,

My Father, What is on Your heart for me today?

I want to become the person You intend for me to be. Help me to be patient as I pursue Your best for my life. Father, You have been faithful to Your Word! Thank You for Your promises, and the fulfillment of those promises in my life.

Amen

"I will bless the Lord, Who has given me counsel; yes, my heart instructs me in the night seasons."
Psalm 16:7 AMP

My Precious Child,

It is a new day. Your life is being transformed from the dust of shattered dreams, bringing forth the promises that I have spoken. My hand of mercy is upon you. All you have experienced shall become the platform upon which you stand, for you have experienced much and grown tremendously. Take refuge in the knowledge that I have a plan for your life. Struggle not with the details, but look to Me. All will come about naturally and be a joy to your heart. Proclaim My goodness, and together we shall see victory!

You Are Blessed,

Your Loving Father

Father,

You have put such hope in my heart. Thank You for touching my life in such a transforming way. Thank You, Father, for Your goodness and steadfast protection! I love You, Father.

Loving Father, I place my life in Your hands and say yes to Your plans for my life!

Amen

"O taste and see that the Lord [our God] is good!
Blessed [happy, fortunate, to be envied] is the
man who trusts and takes refuge in Him."
Psalm 34:8 AMP

Day 195

My Child,

I have such great plans for you. I give you a job to do and you don't always know what follows next. I simply need you to do your best and live your life out with joy and then completely release the cares unto Me. Don't retain the residue of the day's burdens. Small burdens build up into a heavy load. Resist the temptation to judge. That is My job. Where there is happiness and peace, there is no room for a hindered spirit. Break forth this day with a bright spirit. Rejoice in the new day before you and in the freedom that new day promises.

I Love You,

Your Father

Thank You, Loving Father,

Dear Father, Each day is a gift from You. Help me to treasure today.

For letting me be a part of Your wonderful plan. When I'm tempted to hold on to burdens, help me to release them. When I'm tempted to judge, thank You for showing me a better and more productive way in which to live out each day. Thank You, Father, for making Your ways, my ways!

Amen

"Do not judge and criticize and condemn others, so that you may not be judged and criticized and condemned yourselves."
Matthew 7:1 AMP

My Child,

Have you not seen the difference in the times when your spirit is open and when it has been closed to My Spirit? The open spirit absorbs like a sponge without fear and apprehension. The closed spirit responds with a closed mind and fearful heart, and can even become prideful. My hand is on your shoulder, child, like an umbrella. Don't stray out from underneath it through doubt or carelessness. My righteousness will prevail in your life as long as you look to Me.

Listen Closely, My Child,

Your Loving Father

Loving Father,

Thank You for giving me ears to hear and eyes to see Your mighty and glorious truths. I want to know Your voice clearly. I want to walk out my life with confidence, knowing You are going before me, making my path clear.

Father, Open my eyes, Lord, that I might see this day, as You do.

Amen

"*Open my eyes, that I may see*"
Psalm 119:18 NKJV

Day 197

My Child,

Stand your ground and be all that I have created you to be. My truth is stable and the only foundation on which to build. All else is unstable. I have carefully watched over your life. I have paved your way with My Spirit. Take full advantage of this opportunity, for it brings with it promise and achievement, opening the door to victory. Resist all forms of corruptive speech (complaining and criticizing), for it is the opposite of praise. In praise, you will continue to see change and victory in your life.

I Sing Over You With Joy!

Your Loving Father

Dear Father,

Father, How can I better stand true to who You have called me to be and what You have called me to do?

Help me greet each day with joy in who You have created me to be, with happiness in my heart and a smile on my face. Keep Your Presence near and evident to me. Help me, Father, I pray, to start each day, and carry it through, in such a wonderful way.

Amen

"O God, my heart is fixed [steadfast, in the confidence of faith]; I will sing, yes, I will sing praises,"
Psalm 108:1 AMP

My Child,

Don't look back to the past but stand resolved and at peace in the present, released from the hardships of the past. Relax and enjoy the view. I am with you in all things. I will bless you in the stillness, and I will bless you in the times of activity. Now it is a time of forgiveness and the laying down of strife to bring forth a new day of peace. Go forward knowing that I have calmed the waters and brought forth peace. Walk in absolute acceptance and forgiveness with others. Do not demand that they realize wrongs done. Simply accept and go on. I know each and every detail. I know and see, and that is all that is necessary. Free your heart to receive My blessings.

You Are Blessed, My Child,

Your Loving Father

Father,

There is such freedom in loving Your way! With Your way there is no keeping an account of wrongs. For You know, and that is all that matters. My part is to simply follow it through step-by-step as You lead, and having done all, to stand. And when all has been done that can be done, to simply accept and go on, in peace. I love Your ways, Father!

Loving Father, Are there struggles and trials from the past that I need to let go of?

Amen

"Above all things have intense and unfailing love for one another, for love covers a multitude of sins [forgives and disregards the offenses of others]."

1 Peter 4:8 AMP

My Child,

See, the sun is shining. In times of challenge, in the midst of the storm, allow My light to shine even brighter in your life. In times of trouble, I will be your anchor. My strength and righteousness shall shine forth brightly. You are precious to Me. Trust in My unfailing, powerful love. Go forth with singing and hope bubbling up in your heart, for I have made this day for you to enjoy.

Trust In Me, My Child,

Your Loving Father

Father,

You have never let me down. Help me to walk in absolute trust. Thank You for the gift of hope and for shining in my life with happiness for each new day. You are the Light of my life! I love You!

Loving Father, You have always been there for me.

Amen

"I will trust and not be afraid, for the Lord God is my strength and song; yes, He has become my salvation."
Isaiah 12:2 AMP

My Child,

Test your wings today. Fly high. Concentrate on Me and you will discover that together we can catch the high currents. Be constant in My Presence and let Me bring hope to your inner being. Be not concerned; simply be and I shall direct your path. Seek Me and discover Me in ways you've never known before. Celebrate your life with Me each day. Take the wings of hope with abandon. I am with you and together there is nothing we cannot conquer.

Keep Your Heart Expectantly Hopeful,

Your Father

Loving Father,

Nothing is more wonderful than being in Your Presence, knowing You love me, that You have created me to be in intimate fellowship with You, and that together there is nothing we cannot conquer! I will praise You with abandon, knowing that as I worship You, new hope for my life's purpose will arise in my heart. I love You and trust You, Father!

Dear Father, Help me today to place my absolute hope and trust in the plans You have preordained for me.

Amen

"And now, Lord, what do I wait for and expect?
My hope and expectation are in You."
Psalm 39:7 AMP

My Child,

It is your time of rest and restoration—resting from worries and cares. Take refuge in My Presence. Lean back and let Me hold the weight. I will bring you into a high place of serenity and peace. Rejoice, My child, and be glad, for you have faced the enemy and prevailed. Now, rest is imperative; rest in body, soul, and spirit. Measure the need and respond as I lead. I give My beloved rest. The way is clear and moving forward in My timing and at My bidding for a glorious and rewarding life.

Rest, My Child!

Your Loving Father

Loving Father,

Father, I will simply rest in You today.

I'm so used to responding to every need, that I will need Your help to respond as You lead. Thank You, Father, for giving me the grace to know that all will be done in Your time and in Your way. I will simply rest in Your arms, lean back, and let You hold the weight! What a wonderful place to be!

Amen

"My people shall dwell in a peaceable habitation,
in safe dwellings, and in quiet resting-places."
Isaiah 32:18 AMP

My Child,

The way of your life has a purpose and a reason. I am always enveloping you and carrying you forward. I have strengthened you, and I will continue to lead you beside streams of living water. The strain and stress of life shall be transformed into the newness that you have so desired. Relax, let Me fill you, refine you, and polish you for My purposes. Stand ready to march forth with resilience and power in My Name, armed and strengthened by My Spirit and of praises from your heart. Walk toward the bright future I have for you.

Enveloping You With Love,

Your Father

Loving Father,

You continually give hope where there seems to be no hope, peace where there seems to be no peace, and strength and purpose when life gets complex. Thank You, Father, for using every experience of my life to fill, refine, polish, and prepare me for Your purposes. Thank You that You are always there to love and encourage along the way.

Dear Father, My heart is lifted to You with loving praise today!

Amen

*"I will bless the Lord at all times; His praise
shall continually be in my mouth."*
Psalm 34:1 AMP

My Child,

My Spirit hovers over you and is preparing and charging you for the work at hand. Enjoy My closeness! Be released from all doubts and fear, for the path ahead is filled with purpose. Drink in My freshness. Shine forth My radiance. Be once more that beacon to draw the lost to My light and warmth. I send you forth to bring My restoration to others. Lavish it upon them with gentleness. I have strengthened you, empowered you, and sent you forth, knowing who you are in Me.

I Am With You, My Child,

Your Loving Father

Loving Father,

Help me to lead others to You simply by living my life in an honorable manner. Thank You for this glorious journey. I lift up my heart and rejoice in the new day, filled with its joys and treasures from You. I love You, Father!

Father, Thank You for pouring Your love out on me, so that I can share it with others!

Amen

"Let your light so shine before men, that they may see your good works and glorify your Father in heaven."
Matthew 5:16 NKJV

My Child,

No longer will you wonder if I can cover you and protect you. You shall know, and My glory shall be revealed through your life in a new and more powerful way. A reservoir of hope has been building in your heart, pushing out the residue of the past. Look forward to your future. It begins today, and today is bright with the hope and promise of the freedom, power, and blessings from My hand. Rejoice in Me, your Maker! Make it a habit to rejoice in the God of your Salvation! Be encouraged, rejoice in each morning as the days unfold one-by-one, for the destination is sure and the results shall cause you to look at life in a new way…as I do.

Rejoice, My Child,

I Love You

Loving Father,

Thank You for placing a future full of promise before me. And I am thankful, Lord, for renewed hope and encouragement for the journey. Surely my heart exclaims with joy, You are an awesome God, and nothing is too hard for You!

Father, Thank You for restoring to my heart absolute confidence in You!

Amen

"Behold, the Lord's eye is upon those who fear Him [who revere and worship Him with awe], who wait for Him and hope in His mercy and loving-kindness."
Psalm 33:18 AMP

My Child,

Struggle is not necessary. Cast your cares on Me and let Me carry the burden of your frustrations. Be strong, prepared to endure. For I am with you to assure, strengthen, and cheer you on. You will see transformations in your life as your strength returns. You will become more aware of My voice and guidance along the way. Study My Word. Be faithful in the small things and I will bless you abundantly in the big things. Be fearless and go forward, undaunted by the past, but spurred on by the vision given. It truly is a new day, filled with great gain.

Cast Your Cares On Me,

Your Loving Father

Loving Father,

Father, What small things would You have me be faithful in today?

Thank You for Your constant, faithful, and loving care. Thank You, Lord, that I don't have to understand everything, but can simply trust You. Most of all, Father, thank You for renewed vision and recharged strength to go forward in Your love!

Amen

*"Casting the whole of your care [all your anxieties,
all your worries, all your concerns, once and for all]
on Him, for He cares for you affectionately
and cares about you watchfully."*
1 Peter 5:7 AMP

Day 206

My Child,

The gate has swung wide open for you. You shall show others that there is a way out of the wilderness that leads to life, refreshing, and hope. I will show you how to minister hope to those who are thirsty for the Word of Life. Let your life be a representation of Me. My Spirit is upon you to offer abundant life, full and free to others. My hand of restoration and freedom is upon you, and the reality of My love shall be evident in you in a new way. In peace you shall drink from the well of restoration. Your soul shall magnify the Lord and recount His mercies to you, and you shall see and respond to new ways of moving by My Spirit of truth.

It Is A New Day, My Child,

Your Loving Father

Dear Father,

It is so wonderful to know that there is a reason and purpose for our lives. It makes it all worthwhile to know that I can minister hope to Your people and give them the Word of Life that will set them free. Thank You for Your hand of restoration and freedom upon my life. Your gentle love and care are the joy of my life!

Loving Father, Who can I reach out to this day?

Amen

"Now to Him who is able to do exceedingly
abundantly above all that we ask or think,
according to the power that works in us,"
Ephesians 3:20 NKJV

My Child,

Every step you take, I am watching. Though the scene is changing, I am bringing you into a beautiful open plain. My hand is upon you to cause you to flourish and grow. You have been sustained and now you shall flourish. The pieces of your life shall begin to fit together, and you will see a beautiful picture begin to form from out of the chaos. My power to bring it forth is with you, and you shall see mighty miracles by My hand. Go forth this day in joy, for neither fire nor flood have swayed you, and the sunshine and beauty of My Kingdom shall bring healing and restoration unto you. This peace and well being are your inheritance.

I Love You, My Child,

Your Father

Loving Father,

Father, Guide my ways through this day.

Your Presence is precious to me. Through everything You have always been with me, sustaining me and helping me to make the right choices. Thank You for bringing healing, restoration, a sense of peace, and well being into my life. I love You, Father.

Amen

"The steps of a [good] man are directed and established by the Lord when He delights in his way [and He busies Himself with his every step]."
Psalm 37:23 AMP

Day 208

My Child,

Relish the sound of quietness, for there My heart is. My Presence is near. It is My heart you hear in the silence. Streamline your life, that it might be a constant reflection of My love and redemptive power. Trade in all that distracts you for that which calls forth My Spirit in your life. Rejoice in your life. It is a season of change, coming forth with great joy and exuberance. Call it forth!

Relish My Presence!

Your Loving Father

Dear Father,

I want to hear Your voice. Help me to be silent and hear when You speak to me. I want to know You personally. Help me keep my focus on You.

Amen

Loving Father, What steps should I take to effectively streamline my life?

"And the effect of righteousness will be peace [and external], and the result of righteousness will be quietness and confident trust forever."
Isaiah 32:17 AMP

Day 209

My Child,

A season of lightheartedness is upon you, a release from tension brought about by a free fall into My arms of love. It is a strategy of release. Brokenness has brought it about. Sing, My little songbird. Sing for joy. Sing for the joy of My heart. Be released from the struggles of the past. They do not apply today. Let your heart sing. Let your praises ring in the Presence of your King. To God be the glory!

Sing To Me With Joy!

Your Father

Dearest Father,

Father, I will simply enjoy this place in Your care today and listen for Your voice of healing in my heart.

I can envision that free fall into Your arms of love, such a place of safety! What a wonderful place to release the struggles of the past, letting the brokenness be healed in Your care, and to simply sing to You with joy and thankfulness! I love You, Father!

Amen

"Bless [affectionately, gratefully praise] the Lord,
O my soul; and all that is [deepest] within me,
bless His holy name."
Psalm 103:1 AMP

My Child,

Be My light to the world. Pierce the darkness with My light, knowing that in loving one another with a pure heart you are unified and strengthened. Balance freedom with passion, freedom to just be, and passion to do. Great things are coming your way, igniting the fires that have been smoldering your life. There is no reason to stand on the sidelines of life. Be established in this place of blessing and harmony. Be My light to the world.

You Are Free, My Child!

Your Loving Father

Father,

Help me to love others as You do. Thank You, Father, for this place of blessing and harmony! And, Father, thank You for bringing blessing and harmony into my life. I do want to be a blessing to others. Show me how to reach out with compassion and also how to live my life as a bright, shining example.

Precious Father, How would You use me today to shine Your light into this day?

Amen

"For it is the God who commanded light to shine out of darkness, who has shone in our hearts to give the light of the knowledge of the glory of God in the face of Jesus Christ."

2 Corinthians 4:6

My Precious Child,

Don't you know that I hold you in the palm of My hand, and from there I hold you next to My heart? This time of rest shall bear much fruit. You will find that your heart beats with a new desire to tackle things. Let Me fill you once again with newness of life. Let Me sing over you with gladness, and together we shall again go forth with joy and lightness of heart. The best is yet to come. Seek Me each day that your life might again shine brightly. My feast of love and acceptance is yours.

Bask In My Love, My Child,

Your Father

Loving Father,

Precious Father, Today I want to seek You with my whole heart.

I will go through this day with a smile on my face and a song in my heart, loving You with every breath I take! Knowing You are singing over me with gladness causes my heart to fly with joy! Please give me a new song today from Your heart to mine, that I might sing it back to You!

Amen

"You open Your hand and satisfy every living thing with favor."
Psalm 145:16 AMP

My Child,

"Impossible" it has been said. But you will see that by My hand and provision, what seems impossible becomes reality. Tremendous days lie ahead, heralding the fulfillment of your hopes and dreams through doorways yet unseen. Miraculous paths for you to tread, as by My hand, you are led. It shall be said, "She did it God's way!" Stalwart and sure shall your steps be, led by Me, making a sure path across the wilderness into the promised land.

You Are Precious To Me, My Child,

Your Loving Father

Loving Father,

Surely my life has been led by Your hand of love. What an adventure to watch You turn each day into an opportunity. Thank You, Father, for helping me to make the right choices along the way of my life.

Father, I'm listening with anticipation to hear Your Words of direction and love.

Amen

"And [God] Who provides seed for the sower and bread for eating will also provide and multiply your [resources for] sowing and increase the fruits of your righteousness, [which manifests itself in active goodness, kindness, and charity]."
2 Corinthians 9:10 AMP

Day 213

My Child,

Know that you are loved by the Creator of the universe. Far greater is this knowledge than any other on the face of the earth. Rest in that assurance and love. Continue to seek My heart in all things. Strongholds will be broken as you stand in the strength of that love. My heart is with you, to fulfill all I have placed before you. Within your heart are the tools you seek — hidden away, unseen to the naked eye, but readily seen by My Spirit within you. One by one, I shall draw them forth, providing new avenues of service to delight your heart. Let your heart rejoice, for in that rejoicing comes the freedom to soar and to live your life fully.

I Love You, My Child,

Your Father

Loving Father,

Loving Father, Today I want to seek Your heart about:

Help me to remember that You have a plan and destiny for my life. Each day, a treasure revealed by Your spirit of love. Thank You, Father, for the love and encouragement that You give to me and that You bring my way through others.

Amen

"And my spirit rejoices in God my Savior."
Luke 1:47 AMP

My Child,

Many seasons have changed your life. But nestled between the events of life is the assurance of My love and care to keep you stable in the face of turmoil and confusion. Call up memories of past victories and rejoice in each outcome, for I am with you and will never forsake you or leave you without an answer. You've sought My face; you've stood strong. You will see that nothing shall be lost as together we continue on the way, fulfilling your destiny each and every day. Be refreshed this day.

I Am Always With You!

Your Loving Father

Loving Father,

Help me to remember to look to You when my life seems to be getting out of control. There is no place else I'd rather be than fulfilling my destiny, each and every day, in intimate fellowship with You! I love You, Father!

Father, Thank You for the refreshment of Your steadfast love this day!

Amen

"Yes, you shall be steadfast and secure; you shall not fear."
Job 11:15 AMP

My Child,

Trace your life through the many ups and downs, and you'll see that My hand has been upon you at all times, bringing you from trial to victory. So it is now as you see My hand of favor leading you to your predestined blessing. The road has at times been dry and barren — seemingly void of laughter, joy, and fellowship. But now comes a new day to gladden your heart, set you free to sing, and be refreshed in My love. Your heart has become a dwelling place for My love. You cannot fathom the depths of that love. Just let it flow out unhindered by the passing circumstances. I hear your heart. Rest assured that I hear, as you stand before Me.

Be Refreshed In My love,

Your Loving Father

Loving Father,

Father, I turn my heart in trust to You today.

It is amazing to me that You hear every cry of my heart, that You consider every thought and prayer. Teach me how to let go of the daily cares and turn to You with trust. Thank You for giving my life meaning and true purpose.

Amen

"In Him [and in fellowship with one another]
you yourselves also are being built up [into this
structure] with the rest, to form a fixed abode
(dwelling place) of God in (by, through) the Spirit."
Ephesians 2:22 AMP

My Child,

I have written you on the palm of My hand. You are always before My face. Your life is becoming a reflection of Me—full of My beauty and grace. Though you have struggled to maintain the pace, don't let down your guard. I will show you a new life ahead, full of purpose—a life that is satisfying and renewing. Look to Me. You are My dearest treasure, held safely in My hand.

You Are Precious To Me,

Your Loving Father

Loving Father,

Help me, Father, to let go of the daily struggles and to rest in Your love. Bring my heart, daily, to a place of peace. Help me stand with strength in Your Spirit. Each day, show me how to seek out the peace and the serenity that only You can give. Thank You for helping me come to a new place of balancing work and play in my life.

Dear Father, Today I will cast my worries and walk carefree in You!

Amen

"See, I have inscribed you on the palms of My hands;"
Isaiah 49:16 AMP

My Child,

I want to teach you My ways. Meditate on My Word and learn My heart. My ways are revealed through My Word. Reflect on My way. Now is the time to see the future with expectation—through My eyes, eyes of freedom and eternal destiny. Stand with the faith of a small child holding Daddy's hand. Go forth, with a song of freedom in your heart!

Be Free, My Child, Be Free!

Your Loving Father

Loving Father,

Father, Thank You for teaching me Your ways as I meditate on Your Word today.

Thank You for holding tightly to my hand. Day-by-day, You give me glimpses into my destiny, and each give me hope and direction. Thank You for giving me the faith to stand and receive all You have for me. Thank You, Father, for a rising sense of freedom that permeates my heart and soul. I love You, Father!

Amen

"Show me Your ways, O Lord; teach me Your paths."
Psalm 25:4 AMP

My Child,

It is My great pleasure to bless you. Release to Me every pressure of life. Release to Me and gain renewed sight and peace. Within My peace is a full liberation from anxiety, tension, fear, and stress. Come into My rest. My peace is the measure of My life within you. It is peace you experience as you stand in faith and believe. Stand your ground this day, My child. It is holy ground, this place of peaceful habitation with Me.

Be At Peace, My Child,

Your Loving Father

My Father,

How I long to walk in complete peace each day! Truly it is a place of peaceful habitation, this place with You where I am released from anxiety, tension, fear, and stress. What joy there is to walk in Your peace.

Loving Father, Help me to make that choice today to walk in Your trust and peace.

Amen

"For I know the thoughts that I think toward you, says the LORD, thoughts of peace and not of evil, to give you a future and a hope."
Jeremiah 29:11 NKJV

My Child,

Continue to make yourself available to others. Set an atmosphere that they might desire My love and be filled. Proceed along the road that I have created for you, filled with delights and treasures beyond your capacity to comprehend. You shall see My hand of provision at every turn. Continue to delight in Me, walking in My favor and love. You have been patient. You have allowed me to guide your way, knowing that I will preserve you and bring to you My very best.

The Best Is Yet To Come!

Your Loving Father

Father,

Loving Father, I give this day to You.

Knowing Your love, peace, and joy has always been my greatest desire. Please lead my life to a place that pleases You.

Amen

*"But as for that [seed] in the good soil, these are
[the people] who, hearing the Word, hold it fast in
a just (noble, virtuous) and worthy heart, and
steadily bring forth fruit with patience."*
Luke 8:15 AMP

My Precious Child,

I share the secrets of My heart with those who will listen with their hearts—those who respond with obedience and love. It is not a small thing, but a way of life that causes My will to be brought forth on the earth. Listen with your heart and hear My Words of love and encouragement. Receive My blessings upon your life. Walk with Me, My child. Sit with Me awhile. Let Me be the cause of your smile.

Listen With Your Heart, My Child,

Your Father

Loving Father,

The sound of Your voice is the joy of my life. You speak Words of encouragement, love, wisdom, direction, peace, and hope. Daily, You cause the lights to go on in my heart as You help me put the pieces of my life together with understanding and hope. Truly, You are the cause of my smile. I love You, Father!

Father, I am listening for Your direction!

Amen

"But there is a God in heaven Who reveals secrets,"
Daniel 2:28 AMP

My Child,

Be restored this day from the rigors of the battle and from the emotions that haven't found a peaceful landing spot. Let Me anoint the fragmented, frayed areas of your life, and bring a calm to your life that you have not known before because of the constant pressures. I have seen, know, and am cognizant of all that pertains to your life. Nothing goes unseen from My eyes. I have watched as you have stood strong and full of courage. Be blessed this day and know it is My pleasure to fill your life with good things.

I Love You, My Child!

Your Loving Father

Loving Father,

Father, I just want to sit in Your Presence for a while and reflect on the many ways You bless me and those I love!

Thank You for anointing the frayed areas of my life and bringing a calm today. I long to be at peace in Your Presence. Thank You that day-by-day You are bringing that about, as You teach me. Thank You for Your healing in my life. You are precious to me, Father!

Amen

"Grace (favor and spiritual blessing) to you and [heart] peace from God our Father and the Lord Jesus Christ (the Messiah, the Anointed One)."
2 Corinthians 1:2 AMP

My Child,

Search your heart. What do you find there? Is it frustration and weariness? Let it all go—every care, every concern, one step at a time. I see that you are fatigued. It is as if you have been on a long marathon, no longer running but getting up every morning and laboriously taking one weary step at a time with the finish line as the goal. Let it all go. I long for you to run and skip with Me, down the pathway of life. Go forth with faith believing, and in peace receiving My Living Word of hope and healing to your heart and soul. A way has been made for you. My blessings of abundant peace by My Spirit are yours. Go forth proclaiming My blessings to My people.

I Am With You!

Your Father

Loving Father,

Help me to remember that You are with me even through the tough times of life. Thank You for bringing hope and healing to my body, soul, and heart. Thank You for Your continual blessings and miracles in my life!

Father, I need to fill up my heart this day with Your loving Presence!

Amen

*"And as for you, brethren, do not become weary
or lose heart in doing right [but continue
in well-doing without weakening]."*
2 Thessalonians 3:13 AMP

My Precious Child,

I want you to understand and learn many things as you continue to grow. It is My greatest desire to bring you to My banquet table and to bless you. I have a divine plan for your life. I want you to know, it's all a part of My plan to bring you forth victorious. My love for you is great — carry it in your heart. A seed has been planted deep within that causes you to always win. That seed is My love.

I Love You, My Child

Your Loving Father

I love You too, Father,

Loving Father, My heart sings a song of love to You! How can I love You more?

With all my heart! Day-by-day You teach me Your ways with such patience, gentleness, grace, and loving care. You have such confidence in me and always see me through. Nothing surprises You or causes You alarm, as step-by-step You bring me to the fulfillment of Your destiny for me, planned from the foundation of the world. With the Creator of the universe as my Father and Friend, I'm sure to win!

Amen

"He brought me to the banqueting house,
and his banner over me was love [for love
waved as a protecting and comforting banner
over my head when I was near Him]."
Song of Solomon 2:4 AMP

My Child,

You will find that fires of life disappear just as quickly as they flare, when you walk with Me as your companion. These fires may be distracting, but they will not harm you. Go forth in My strength and at My leading. Restoration continues to be yours! Don't be afraid of the fires along the way. I am here to protect you. Hold tightly to My hand. These trying times will not devour you. Walk bravely and remain confident in your life. Stride, chin up, in trust that I have a plan for your life.

Trust Me, My Child,

Your Loving Father

Thank You, Father,

For helping me to remember to not let the distracting fires of life set me back. I will trust You to protect my way. Thank You for added strength and restoration as I face my future with renewed confidence.

Father, I will turn my struggles over to You.

Amen

"When you pass through the waters, I will be with you;
And through the rivers, they shall not overflow you.
When you walk through the fire, you shall not
be burned, Nor shall the flame scorch you."
Isaiah 43:2 NKJV

My Beloved Child,

My love is like a stream that spreads across the land, soaking into the dry and parched soil, reviving, restoring, and renewing, with care. My love brings rest to the weary and joy to the downhearted. You are My greatest treasure—a gift of My love. Blessed are our moments together in fellowship. They are yours until they become my eternal gift of love to the world.

I Love You,

Your Loving Father

Precious Father,

Father, Help me to understand, even more, the fullness of Your wonderful love.

My life has, indeed, been healed by Your restoring love! Your Presence brings such joy, victory, and purpose to my very existence. What an awesome and wonderful realization! Thank You, Father, for Your unconditional and life-changing love.

Amen

*"By this we know love, because He laid down
His life for us...."*
1 John 3:16 NKJV

My Child,

Reach out to Me. Focus your heart and affection on Me, and I will orchestrate the rest, bestowing favor and providing all you could have ever hoped for. When your attention becomes sidetracked with the daily responsibilities, all of life becomes out of sync and the harmony intended is lost. It is I Who brings unity and a beautiful composition to your life. Be blessed, this day, as you become lost in the beauty of My music.

Be My Symphony Of Praise!

Your Father

Loving Father,

When I get sidetracked by responsibilities, even in ministry to those You've given me favor with, thank You for gently drawing me back into Your Presence. How wonderful to realize that my life is a predestined and beautiful composition of Your design. As I turn my heart to You, Father, I place my trust and faith in Your hands.

My Father, Today I want to follow the beautiful composition You have written for my life.

Amen

"Direct your heart to the Lord and serve Him only,"
    1 Samuel 7:3 AMP

My Child,

There is much in store. Ready yourself by trusting in Me, absolutely. Come into My Presence. Place your heart in safe keeping with Me. Take refuge in me when you are weary. Lay down, at My feet, every care, My weary child. Take in the beautiful fragrance of time spent with Me. It is a fragrance that lasts and permeates the heart with the beauty of My Spirit around you. It is a facet of My glory. Saturate yourself in My Presence. Let My Presence be your passion! The majesty of My Kingdom is before you. It's music sings in your heart. My hand reaches for your heart. Listen quietly. Only the open heart can hear, for the receiving heart joins with the music of Heaven.

Take Refuge In My Presence,

Your Loving Father

Loving Father,

Father, Forgive me for allowing my soul to become weary. Today I will take refuge in You.

Your Presence truly is the reality of my existence. It is settled in my heart this day. I want to open my heart to You as never before. My heart longs to take refuge in Your Presence! I love You so much, Father!

Amen

"In the Lord, I take refuge [and put my trust];"
Psalm 11:1 AMP

My Child,

Be at peace and know that nothing can overcome you. Simply close the door to the distractions. I have set a course for you. But first you have to be free. Simplicity will continue to be the road map of your life. Frustration comes when priorities get out of order. Simplicity is a grace and a blessing—a gift from Me. Resist the enemy's way of complication and confusion. Remember to keep all things simple and uncomplicated. Avoid division and disappointment.

Stay Free, My Child,

Your Father

Thank You, Father,

For Your gift of simplicity and blessing. Father, every day is a feast from Your table of life, not to be forgotten or taken for granted. Thank You, Father, for Your constant and infinite care, love, and provision over my life!

Loving Father, What are the areas in my life that I need to simplify?

Amen

"Therefore if the Son makes you free,
you shall be free indeed."
John 8:56 NKJV

My Child,

You have used what I have given you and multiplied it to the best of your ability. Now the doors shall swing wide, with more than enough from My storehouses. The time of My favor has come, and upon you I shall pour out the riches of Heaven. Get ready for a flood of My favor and blessing. Your eyes are opening and seeing more clearly. Along with this sight comes wisdom. My house is built with love and wisdom. Give it forth liberally. Liberally I give to you so that liberally you can give to others. The storehouses of Heaven are opening wide. Stand under the outpouring of blessing and rejoice as you see the desires of your heart come to pass!

You Have Done Well, My Child,

Your Loving Father

I love You so much, Father!

Father, Your encouragement means so much to me!

Thank You for giving me the desires of my heart and for the promise of Your abundant blessings over my life. Thank You, Father, for opening my eyes that I might see more of You and receive more of Your wisdom. I am so grateful!

Amen

"Grace (favor and spiritual blessing) and [heart] peace from God the Father and the Lord Christ Jesus our Savior."
Titus 1:4 AMP

My Child,

It is a time of refreshing. A time of coming into My peace. A time of knowing that My love for you is great beyond your expectations. Don't look at your current situation. Look instead to Me. Struggles will come, but My protection and power in your life will always be greater. Stay in My peace and in a place of rest and trust.

Be At Peace, My Child,

Your Loving Father

Loving Father,

I want to grow in peace and love through absolute trust in You. Show me daily how to walk it out step-by-step. Thank You for Your many blessings upon my life. Thank You that no matter what is going on in my life, You are always there to help me to respond to life's pressures with peace.

Father, Once again I come to You, seeking that place of rest and abiding.

Amen

*"His favor is for life; Weeping may endure for
a night, But joy comes in the morning."
Psalm 30:5 NKJV*

Precious One,

My promises to you are at hand. You are not standing on shifting sand, but are strong and secure with a heart that is steadfast. Comfort, guidance, and love are always yours, My child. Look to Me for them all, before you ever call upon others to lighten your load. Seasons have brought change over and over again. Now in the midst of it all the answers your heart has longed for has come. I am a faithful Father. My promises are unfaltering; My Word unfailing. Look to Me and allow hope to come alive in your heart as never before.

I Love You!

Your Faithful And Loving Father!

Father,

Loving Father, I just want to enjoy Your Presence today.

You have always been faithful to me! It's not always as I thought it would be, yet each day is filled with Your love and blessing. Help me to hold steady when life gets tough. Thank You, Father, that every moment of my life is a step closer to the magnificence You intended it to be.

Amen

"Let us hold fast the confession of our hope without wavering, for He who promised is faithful."
Hebrews 10:23 NKJV

My Child,

It is a new day. A new beginning. An opportunity to love and appreciate those I have put into your life. Walk in harmony with one another and see each other as I do—full of promise and potential. You are My children—a part of eternity. I've given each of you different abilities and talents. Walk out your gifts and callings reflecting the beauty of a life whole and complete—upon those who have become discouraged and weary. It is My Spirit which sets free the troubled heart. Reflect My love and be a part of the Heavenly song that will ring throughout eternity and bring hope to the world.

Be My Song Of Hope, My Child,

Your Father

Beloved Father,

Help me to become sensitive to those around me, that I would always speak words of hope and encouragement. Help me to reflect Your beauty to those You have trusted me with. Help me to always reflect Your love and offer Your healing and renewing touch to those around me.

Loving Father, Who can I reach out to this day with an encouraging act of kindness?

Amen

"[And aim at and pursue] faith, love, [and] peace, harmony and concord with others in fellowship with all [Christians], who call upon the Lord out of a pure heart."
2 Timothy 2:22 AMP

My Precious Child,

It is the journey of a lifetime, a gift from above. It is all about My favor, love, and blessing. Let others run the race at their own pace. Each has an individual purpose and plan. But together, My purpose becomes clear; see the kaleidoscope. There is beauty in every image portrayed. The colors are all connected as they weave in and out, forming beautiful creations. Ever changing but always a wonderful image of symmetry and grace. All necessary to the whole though each are unique. Yes, I have made you beautifully and wonderfully unique.

You Are A Treasure To My Heart,

Your Father

Loving Father,

My Father, Thank You that I am a part of that kaleidoscope of Your precious people. Cause me to love them even more!

Thank You for Your blessing on my life and for filling it with Your favor and love. Thank You for Your guiding hand, which leads my life as You have preordained. Your grace is a blessing in my life, filling it with purpose and meaning.

Amen

*"Yet grace (God unmerited favor) was given
to each of us individually…"*
Ephesians 4:7 AMP

My Child,

It is My pleasure to bring freedom to the world. Walk in that freedom which is yours for the taking. Let My freedom release their hearts. Let the truth of My awesome power ring. Share it with those around you. Truth spoken brings forth the promises of life. Truth spoken calms the struggle of the weary heart. My truth—My Word—brings life! Know that I am your refuge and place of safety. Triumph abides in Me. It's a new day. Proclaim My freedom far and wide, knowing I will always walk by your side. It is My great pleasure to bring freedom and a carefree heart into your life.

Stay Free, My Child, Stay Free!

Your Father

Beloved Father,

Freedom is only found in Your Presence! Freedom is only found in Your love and in Your Name. Please help me walk out my life in such a way that others see Your heart.

Loving Father, How can I walk in more freedom of heart today?

Amen

> *"He has sent me to heal the broken hearted,*
> *To proclaim liberty to the captives,*
> *And the opening of the prison to those who are bound;"*
> Isaiah 61:1 AMP

Day 235

My Child,

Blessed, you are blessed! Welcome into My Presence. You are loved beyond measure. Joy is yours to proclaim, as you walk in My love and in the power of My Name! Peace permeates your soul, because you know I have full control in every circumstance. You can trust My heart. Let your fears and reluctance just evaporate. I am the best friend you'll ever have. Feast at My table. My love for you will never decline. You are Mine!

Proudly, I Say, You Are Mine!

Your Loving Father

Dear Father,

You are the best friend I've ever had! What a privilege to dine at Your table of blessing. My life is rich and full because of Your powerful love.

Loving Father, I just want to pour out my love on You today with thankfulness and praise!

Amen

"But as for me, I will enter Your house through the abundance of Your steadfast love and mercy;"
Psalm 5:7 AMP

Day 236

My Child,

In the midst of heartbreak comes the sound of a dove singing songs of love. Can you not hear its sweet song, refreshing like soft, gentle rain? Listen to its beautiful refrain. It is My song of love that moves the heart. It's the sweetness of that song that causes others to feel a part of My plan and purpose upon the earth, where before they felt discarded or alone. My song of love, you see, brings forth hope causing the brokenness to flee. Precious and few are those who do proclaim My love in such a way that brings forth My blessing through what they do and say! So, sing My song in your heart. Let it bring forth every freedom, deliverance, and hope. Let your heart sing My song of liberty. Be delivered and made whole.

Sing, My Child,

Your Father

Loving Father,

You've given me a beautiful song in my heart. Please help me to enter Your Presence with that great gift of renewed hope, faith, and trust. It is an incredible gift to be able to enter Your Presence, receive Your forgiveness, and walk out each day with You by my side.

Father, Teach me of Your love today.

Amen

"O sing to the Lord a new song,
for He has done marvelous things;"
Psalm 98:1 AMP

When God Speaks to My Heart

My Beloved Child,

I have put it on your heart, year after year, "Love each other with a pure heart, untainted by expectations or goals, simply for love's sake." Now, I say to you that love shall bear fruit beyond your expectations or dreams. It is a message whose time has come. The Kingdom of God is gladness, love, and purity. As you walk through life you will see My hand of favor, joy, and love covering all with hope and peace. Go forth under My canopy of love.

You Are Precious To Me,

Your Loving Father

Loving Father,

Father, Who can I reach out to today with Your love?

Through the years Your compassion has been abundantly evident in my life. Help me to walk in that special and divine love for those You have placed in my world. Sometimes it's easy, sometimes it's hard, but always the rewards are great. Thank You, Father, for teaching me to love!

Amen

"A friend loves at all times,"
Proverbs 17:17 AMP

My Child,

When you are weary, come to Me. Come to Me and listen to the sound of My heart, the music of the spheres, to bring you joy and lighten your heart. Listen to its gentle refrain; it's never the same and it brings release. My heart for you, My child, sings a song of freedom! Freedom from disappointment and weariness of heart—freedom to know that every day you are a part of My will and plan upon the earth. Be at peace, My child, and release a song of praise unto Me. Each day come into My Presence and partake in worship with the Heavenlies, a symphony of praise unto Me, and experience great blessing.

I Love You, My Child,

Your Father

Loving Father,

I want to sing my song of praise to You. I want to sit at Your throne, singing a symphony of praise with love. Thank You, Lord, for helping me continue to grow, destined to be a part of Your will and plan upon the earth—a symphony of love from Your heart!

Wonderful Father, My heart sings to You with gratefulness and love!

Amen

*"I will sing of mercy and loving-kindness
and justice; to You, O Lord, will I sing."*
Psalm 101:1 AMP

Day 239

My Child,

Signs of spring are everywhere. It is a season of new beginnings, new illuminations, resolutions, and victories won. Rise up, My dear one, and sing the song of spring. I lay before you the steps to take, to lead you down the straight path of My choosing. Sing and rejoice daily on this journey. Though the progress seems small at times, know that each day brings you closer to the goal, your destiny is in Me. Faint not, but continue on, knowing that I am with you in every detail of life. Multitudes have come this way without the will and heart to stay. It's all about trust!

I Love You,

Your Father

Loving Father,

Even though the progress seems small at times, I know I can trust You! Thank You, Father, for Your faithful encouragement along the way, so that I don't lose sight of the goal!

Faithful Father, Thank You, for being with me in every detail of my life.

Amen

"And the effect of righteousness will be peace
[internal and external], and the result of righteousness
will be quietness and confident trust forever."
Isaiah 32:17 AMP

My Dear One,

Now is the day! Now is the hour to come into My Presence. Open your heart to Me. I long to spend time with you. It is a time to heal and grow. Now is the hour to stretch forth your hand and receive every blessing awaiting you. Extinguish fear. Extinguish reluctance. You're released this very hour! Go forth proclaiming My love and My grace to those around you—that they too might experience My love.

You Are Precious To Me,

Your Loving Father

Dear Father,

I am in anticipation of what You have planned for my life. As I hang on to my dreams, I go forth with Your promises ringing in my heart. Help me to leave behind all that encumbers my thought life, that I would focus through trust and reliance on You.

Loving Father, What are we going to do together today?

Amen

"I will sing of the mercy and loving-kindness of the Lord forever; with my mouth will I make known Your faithfulness from generation to generation."
Psalm 89:1 AMP

Day 241

My child,

The reason you've been put on the earth is to know My Presence. Heart to heart, My Presence is made known. The beat of My heart, is the cadence to follow. Be alert every day of your life, and you will recognize loud and clear the sound of My love falling on your ear. It's a distinctive sound; it cannot be duplicated. Through intimacy with Me, you will come to know My voice well.

You Are Precious To Me,

Your Loving Father

Loving Father,

Precious Father, I want to enjoy the wonderful sound of Your love falling on my ear today!

It's wonderful to know that Your canopy of love covers and protects me in every situation. Please make Your Presence and love known to me. I want to come into rest and intimacy with You. Lead me daily, closer to You.

Amen

"For blessed (happy, fortunate, to be envied)
are those who keep my ways."
Proverbs 8:32 AMP

My Child,

Be at peace. Just as the trees have different seasons of growth, so do you. A tree may be surrounded by people or it may be isolated away in the forest, but neither has anything to do with its growth. As long as its Father is providing sunshine, water, and nutrients, it grows in beauty and strength. It depends on the Father's care, not on outside stimulation or influences. So are you to be, the strong, beautiful tree of My planting, nurtured by Me, drawing your source of life and growth from Me. There is a time for outside stimulation and sharing, and there is a time for quiet fellowship and communion with Me.

You Are My Treasure,

Your Loving Father

Loving Father,

I love our time of quiet fellowship and communion! Show my heart how to follow after You step-by-step, for I seek to know the leading of Your heart. My heart is listening.

Father, I am listening for Your Word to my heart today.

Amen

"And let the peace of God rule in your hearts,"
Colossians 3:15 NKJV

My Child,

Take the seasons as they come and rejoice in each. Respond to My love flowing out to you. Soak it up, as a flower soaks up the rays of the sun. Without those vital times of taking in the rays of the sun, the flower becomes stunted. So quiet seasons are necessary to the growth of My children, if they are to become solidly based. Be a strong, solid stalk who has steadily soaked in the sun. Rejoice in our quiet time together.

You Are Precious To Me,

Your Loving Father

Father,

Father, What treasures do You have in Your Word for me today?

I want to be that strong, solid stalk who has steadily soaked in the sun, soaked in Your love. I want to feed on Your Word night and day. It is life to me. Speak to me, Lord. I am listening.

Amen

"Pray to your Father who is in the secret place; and your Father who sees in secret will reward you openly."
Matthew 6:6 NKJV

My Child,

Be at peace. Do the flowers of the fields struggle to receive the beauty of their raiment? No, they trust in their Father's care and receive in due season. So shall it be with you. Struggle not and be at peace, for in My time and at My command, each piece shall fall into place and come to pass as I have set forth. Do not be disturbed by what seems a lack of productive activity. Even the beautiful flower must lie dormant in the field until spring. But then it arises to new life and beauty. So be not perplexed nor puzzled by your situation, drawing strength and taking each day as it dawns, with joy and thanksgiving. For My Spirit shall be manifested in abundant ways that you know not of, and you shall rejoice with Me as it is revealed.

Be At Peace, My Child,

Your Loving Father

Father,

Thank You for Your loving encouragement in the different seasons of my life. It brings such comfort to know You walk through each season with me! I know You will never desert me or forsake me. Your ways bring peace no matter what the surrounding circumstances may be.

Loving Father, I am coming into Your Presence today to draw on Your strength and Your peace. Speak to my heart, I pray!

Amen

"In due time and at the appointed season we shall reap,
if we do not loosen and relax our courage and faint."
Galatians 6:9 AMP

Day 245

Dear One,

Lay before My feet your desires and your pursuits. Let Me handle the plans and lead the way. My plans come forth with much fruit. Don't be afraid to express your desires to Me. Give them to Me; leave them with Me. Your heart will rejoice to see how I bring just the right things to pass. So bring every care, every hope to Me. Lay them on the altar, and go your way in peace.

Trust Me, My Child,

Your Loving Father

I Love You, Father!

Loving Father, These are the desires that I have held to my heart. I want to share them with You.

So often I just hold my desires to my own heart and forget to share them with You. I do trust You, Father, and want to share everything that's on my heart with abandon, because You are my loving Father!

Amen

"Many plans are in a man's mind, but it is the Lord's purpose for him that will stand."
Proverbs 19:21 AMP

My Child,

The prize is won in the natural by sacrifice, determination, and endurance. The same is true of the spiritual realm. Be faithful to the calling on your life, and you shall be the recipient of great reward. Continue on! Don't let up in your quest for wisdom. Hand in hand, walk with Me! Every good thing I have shall be yours. Seek after My heart. Knock at My door and I shall have the door opened to you and you shall enter in with joy. Continue your quest, for your reward is sure.

The Best Is Yet To Come!

Your Loving Father

Loving Father,

The desire of my heart has always been to know You more each day, to have Your wisdom and blessing and to hear Your voice more clearly. Thank You, Father, for showing me the way to walk out my journey of this life in a manner pleasing to You. Give me endurance, that I would persevere to the places and callings You have intended for me.

I love You, Father! Thank You for speaking to my heart!

Amen

"And your ears will hear a word behind you, saying,
This is the way; walk in it, when you turn to the
right hand and when you turn to the left."
Isaiah 30:21 AMP

My Child,

I have heard your many prayers as you have entered into intimate time with Me. Receive My healing Words into your heart. Let the Words of My Spirit ring forth with clarity and truth. Cling to them with ever increasing vigil, for they are strength to your heart and everlasting life to your soul. Remain in My love forever. Release unto Me your disappointments. You are not forgotten during this time in the desert. I am ever near to strengthen and prepare you. I will send you out with power and with My Word and with My Spirit. Become one with Me!

You Are Blessed, My Child,

Your Loving Father

Loving Father,

Precious Father, I want You to have total access to my heart.

It is so easy to feel alone during the hard times. Thank You for reminding me that it is a time to be strengthened in You, to become one with You. Teach me through my time of reading Your Words over and over again, for they truly bring renewed life to my heart and my soul. I love You, Father!

Amen

"O Lord, You have heard the desire and the longing
of the humble and oppressed; You will prepare
and strengthen and direct their hearts,
You will cause Your ear to hear."
Psalm 10:17 AMP

My Child,

There is no area in your life that My love cannot touch and re-create. Draw on My love. Depend on My love. And as you do this, that same love will flow from you to others. That drawing and dependence on My love creates a flow from Me, to you, to others: a flow that is continuous. So continue to draw and depend on My love, that others in need might be healed and restored. Beauty and strength come through My love. All gifts of My Spirit are created by My love. So are your gifts to be, created through My pure love given forth. Stand firm, stand tall in My love, for you are My beloved child, in whom I am well pleased!

Be My Love!

Your Loving Father

Dear beloved Father,

Receiving and giving Your love means everything to me! Today, I find myself surrounded by Your Presence. Your love is my life. The power of Your love is amazing.

Amen

Loving Father, I love You with all my heart. Being in Your loving Presence is the joy of my life!

"And above all these [put on] love and enfold yourselves with the bond of perfectness [which binds everything together completely in ideal harmony]."
Colossians 3:14 AMP

Day 249

My Child,

I have designed a wonderful plan for your life and My desire is to help you find that plan in every moment. As you seek my guidance, I will gladly give you direction. When you feel you are running up against a wall in the maze of life, remember to call on Me. I will pour out My wisdom and My mercy so that you are able to overcome every trial. Depending on Me contains the promise of success and victory. The more you learn to lean on Me, the easier your way will become. Depend on My guidance.

Your Loving Father

Loving Father,

Father, I love Your Presence, and I love depending on You to lead me in every decision.

As I learn to follow Your leading in my heart, I am beginning to understand that I can be precise in my decisions. When You are directing me, the enemies of my soul begin to flee. You cause me to be right on time, not too early and not too late. Thank You for giving me the encouragement to do what I need to do, knowing that the outcome is secure. What a wonderful way to live, Father, following Your leading and guidance.

Amen

"You will guide me with Your counsel, and afterward receive me to honor and glory."
Psalms 73:24 AMP

My Child,

I have given you the choice to live in abundance; but it requires discipline, obedience, and communion with Me. You can walk a life full of blessings, if you seek after My ways. I will not violate your will to choose what you want in this life. If you choose My ways of love and peace, blessings will come abundantly to you. But if you choose your own way, you will open the door for heartache and difficulties. Do not strive for greatness and pleasure, but seek Me first and My ways in your every day life. Then My blessings will come without sorrow and the desires of your heart will be yours.

Listen To My Heart,

Your Loving Father

My Father,

I set my heart to choose Your ways and to seek Your face. You told me in Your Word that You would show me the path of life and that in Your Presence is fullness of joy.

I choose Your comfort and guidance, joy and refreshing. I choose Your destiny for my life with Your perfect timing. I love You, my Father, and I trust You!

Loving Father, I will seek Your ways all of my days. You bring me a joy that no one can ever take away.

Amen

"Behold, I set before you this day
a blessing and a curse."
Deuteronomy 11:26 AMP

My Child,

The light of My Word will uncover the secrets of people that lead you down the wrong path. Let My truth reveal to you those things that entangle your thoughts and confuse your way. As you spend time in My Word, I will reveal Myself to you. You will find treasures that you have not yet imagined. You will find truth that will set you free in your mind, in your spirit, and in your physical being. My salvation will leave you with nothing missing and nothing broken. My Spirit will lead you as you seek goodness and truth. Practice My Presence with ever increasing determination and joy in receiving from Me, My truth, My Word, and the fulfillment of My love.

Walk In Truth,

Your Father

Loving Father,

Precious Father, To stay in Your Word is my desire.

Thank You that Your light and truth lead me through the trying times of my life. Walking into a place that does not acknowledge You is a very cold and lonely experience. But because You are always with me, I trust You to bring me through these difficulties even when I cannot feel You near. Your forgiveness, Your mercy, Your grace, and Your amazing love are where I am at peace. I will seek You in Your Word, and I will seek You with my heart. I desire Your light and Your truth to lead me always.

Amen

"O send out Your light and Your truth,
let them lead me;"
Deuteronomy 11:26 AMP

My Child,

Discard the seeds of unrest in your life, so they are not given room to grow. Love and peace is the key. Give forth of My Spirit through love, peace, and forgiveness. Remember to smooth the way with compassion and loving acceptance. The walls that have held you back will come tumbling down, and your life will overflow with the added blessings of harmony and a propensity of acceptance. Reach out to those around you with acceptance. Let your words be words of encouragement. Blessed is the one who can lay down the right to acknowledgment to bring forth the acknowledgment of another.

Give Forth Of My Love,

Your Loving Father

Father,

Lord, help me always be sensitive to the needs of those You have placed in my life. Help me to refrain from critical thinking or defensive words in an attempt to save face. Instead, show me the way to see others, as You see them. Help me to walk in absolute love, acceptance, and forgiveness. Help me to receive this important life lesson.

Father, Help me always to offer love and acceptance as You have given it to me.

Amen

"Let him search for peace (harmony;
undisturbedness from fears, agitating passions,
and moral conflicts) and seek it eagerly."
1 Peter 3:11 AMP

My Child,

Come to Me. Spend time with Me. Lay down your troubled heart and come to rest. Don't concern yourself with feeling "worthy enough." Just be with Me! Take rest in My wholeness. Let Me pour My love and acceptance out upon you. Plunge headlong into the joy of your salvation, lacking in nothing. Rejoice in each day and its opportunities. A rejoicing heart cannot be easily shaken. Come into My Presence and receive My refreshing. Go forth this day with a thankful heart—singing praises to delight us both!

I Love You!

Your Father

Father,

Loving Father, My ear is tuned in to hear You speak to my heart today.

Father, I do want to know You intimately and personally. Thank You for touching my life with goodness. My heart does sing Your praise in thankfulness. Your love for me is constant and sure!

Amen

"I will rejoice in You and be in high spirits;
I will sing praise to Your name, O Most High!"
Psalm 9:2 AMP

My Child,

Confidence in Me is the key, and the knowledge of My love and confidence in you. Many times you shall hear words that would have detained your heart before or caused you pain. But now those same words shall be brushed aside and replaced with Mine. You shall go forward in your life triumphantly as I lead, in the confidence, power, and authority of your God!

Be Confident In Me!

Your Loving Father

Loving Father,

Thank You, Father, for cleansing my heart of all hurt and rejection. Thank You for filling my life with peace and Your supernatural renewal. Help me to love openly and without fear of rejection. Help me tear down the walls of my life, that I might walk complete and whole in Your care.

Loving Father, I pray that true confidence in You and Your love will always lead me!

Amen

"Therefore let us pursue the things which make for peace and the things by which one may edify another."
Romans 14:19 NKJV

My Child,

Seek My peace. Search for its richness and fulfillment. Take My peace upon your life. Trust in My ways and My hand, which is upon you. Trust My promises. They are yours. Be transformed in My Presence. Receive My love and My peace. Let the fire of understanding light your way, through your constant and persistent peace in Me.

With Love,

Your Father

Father,

Faithful Father, Show me Your peace today.

Thank You for teaching me to walk in peace, day-by-day and moment-by-moment. Thank You for forgiving me when I become anxious. Help me to remember to return to Your Presence and to come right back into that place of peace, calm, and trust when my life encounters the storm. Thank You for Your laughter and joy in my life.

Amen

"You will keep him in perfect peace, whose mind is stayed on You, because he trusts in You."
Isaiah 26:3 NKJV

My Precious One,

You have faced the wind and come out strong. The weight of the world has fallen from your shoulders that you might fly with freedom, restored by the might of My power and love. You have turned a corner, walking in My favor. It shall bring forth added truth and sustenance for your soul and spirit. Fear not about tomorrow. Go forth with a song in your heart and a song of praise on your lips, for My Word in your life has prevailed.

You Are Precious To Me,

Your Loving Father

I Love You, Father!

You have brought me such a long way by the power of Your love. There is such a freedom in walking with You, and simply walking out my life with a song of praise on my lips for You, my faithful and loving Father and God!

Loving Father, Thank You for this hope:

Amen

"For He spoke, and it was done;
He commanded, and it stood fast."
Psalm 33:9 AMP

My Child,

Be My peacemaker. Walk your life out daily with the blessings I have offered you. I have turned your mourning into joy, your sadness into thanksgiving, and given to you blessings evermore. Stand on the Rock of My Salvation. Forsake not your stance of thanksgiving, for unto you have I poured out my wealth of blessings. Don't fear what may lie ahead, for My blessing awaits you. For unto those who seek My will, I've made manifest the wonders of My Kingdom. Nothing can deter you from your appointed walk with Me. Nothing can shatter, scatter, nor detract from the wholeness of the walk I have appointed for you to walk in.

You Are Precious To Me!

Your Loving Father

Loving Father,.

Father, Here I am, loving the peace of Your Presence and seeking Your will about:

Thank You that no matter how fierce the storm or how confusing the situation, You are there, bringing peace and faith to keep walking forward. Thank You, Father, for helping me to remain a peacemaker despite the surrounding circumstances. I do love You, Father!

Amen

"Blessed are the peacemakers: for they shall be called the children of God."
Matthew 5:9

My Child,

Many times I have cradled you in My arms and comforted you. Many times you have looked to Me to rescue and tenderly protect you. Know that I have not wavered from My promises to you. One-by-one they have found a place in your life and in your heart as you have believed with an unfaltering faith. This is My gift to you—strength in the midst of the storm, light in the midst of the darkness, and a hope that transcends all doubt. Surely My loving-kindness has anchored you. So now, go forth unafraid, rejoicing in My might, for it is yours; perceiving, receiving, and committing all that you have and are into My loving care. I have brought you into the vast and unending knowledge of My love for you. Go forth with soundness and wholeness of heart, for I am with you.

I Love You, My Child,

Your Father

Loving Father,

Throughout my life You have been there for me. Just the thought of You brings peace to my inner being. When the crisis of the moment overwhelms me, You are there. I depend on Your promises, as one by one they come into view and into reality, to the joy of my heart. Help me to remember that You never give up on me and will always see me through!

Father, Today I look to You for:

Amen

"The words and promises of the Lord are pure words, like silver refined in an earthen furnace, purified seven times over."
Psalm 12:6 AMP

My Child,

Be strong in Me. Walk confidently in your life with fortitude to persevere, and persevere you shall. Come and we shall see triumph through to the very end. Victory through many a challenge and strength of will shall be yours as you look to Me. Go forth with determination to be an overcomer in My Name.

I Am Your Strength!

Your Loving Father

Thank You, Father,

For making me an overcomer in Your Name, with the determination and fortitude to persevere. Thank You for teaching me that You have created me to triumph in life, through You, in all situations. Thank You for being my strength!

Loving Father, Thank You for bringing strength to my heart.

Amen

"The way of the Lord is strength and a stronghold to the upright."
Proverbs 10:29 AMP

My Child,

Keep your focus on Me. With your focus firmly planted on Me, nothing can move you off course, I want to work in your life. I desire success for your life. Don't look to the externals, but to Me. Heed well My Words to you and keep your focus and My ways, for you shall be clear and on track. Keep your attention steady on Me. We shall prevail together.

You Can Trust Me,

Your Father

Father,

When my mind starts circling away from You and Your Word, onto the problems of life, help me remember that Your Word reaches far beyond the moment it is spoken. I choose to keep my focus on You and Your Word, so that we can prevail together. My heart is focused on You.

Loving Father, I am listening with anticipation.

Amen

*"Rooted and built up in Him and established
in the faith, as you have been taught,
abounding in it with thanksgiving."*
Colossians 2:7 NKJV

My Child,

My children cannot fail. If you believe in Me — My love and protection, nothing can come nigh you but My love and peace. You will never be put to shame. Your trust brings forth My promises. Nothing can alter the course of a trusting heart. Trust Me! Trust Me as a carefree child being carried in your Father's arms. No course of action can derail you. There is no power greater than My power. Relax in My love for you.

Trust Me, My Child,

Your Loving Father

Loving Father,

Faithful Father, I bring to You the areas in my life that I need to walk with more trust.

You have touched my life with blessing and precision. Help me to always react with perfect confidence in Your guiding hand. Father, what comfort to know that I cannot fail. I choose to trust You!

Amen

"For the Lord your God is a merciful God;
He will not fail you...."
Deuteronomy 4:31 AMP

My Child,

Seasons change, and with the change in seasons comes a new direction, a new goal, and a new purpose in My Kingdom. Hardship is the birthplace and foundation for victory, My kind of victory. Be not dismayed, but stand tall in the blessing and glory of My acceptance and love, and watch Me bring forth triumph into your life. My Word will raise you up in glorious life; life abundant, everlasting, and free. Stay close to My heart and watch Me work.

You Are Safe In Me!

Your Loving Father

Beloved Father,

Time after time, You have been my refuge. A strong bulwark of peace and stability. You have never forsaken me. Father, thank You for new seasons, new direction, new goals, and new purposes in my life. I love You, Father!

Loving Father, Thank You for Your constant and abiding care over my life.

Amen

*"Unless a grain of wheat falls into the earth and dies,
it remains [just one grain; it never becomes more
but lives] by itself alone. But if it dies, it produces
many others and yields a rich harvest."*
John 12:24 AMP

My Child,

Judging, even in the wrappings of love and concern, is still judging. When you see a challenge in another's life, unrecognized by them, lift it up to Me and leave it there. Don't take the problem upon your own shoulders. It was never meant to rest there. It will weigh you down your heart. Turn those you love over to Me. Allow Me to touch the situation with My awesome, transforming power.

I Love You,

Your Father

Loving Father,

Dear Father, I come to You with trust and faith.

Help me to speak only positive, uplifting words about others and leave the negative unspoken. Show me how to release those I love into Your care and trust You for the rest.

Amen

"And why worry about a speck in your friend's eye,
when you have a log in your own?"
Matthew 7:3 NLT

My Precious Child,

I have fashioned you for joy, to bring forth the harvest! The joy of My Presence causes you to glow. Others can simply look at you, and know I am real! As you bask in My Presence, it shows! Continue in this special way of taking in My joy and Presence every day! The rewards of a joyful, loving heart have no end. There is always something new around the bend to delight your heart! You are blessed beyond measure.

I Love You, My Child!

Your Loving Father

Precious Father,

I do feel blessed beyond measure! Truly every day is filled with new, unexpected delights, brought forth by Your hand of love. I love You so much, Father!

Amen

Loving Father, How can I share Your joy with someone today?

"The harvest truly is plentiful, but the laborers are few. Therefore pray the Lord of the harvest to send out laborers into His harvest."
Matthew 9:37-38 NKJV

My Blessed One,

I will bring peace where there is no peace. You have weathered the storms well. Now I say unto you, be strong, be brave, be bold. Speak forth My Word with power, love, and truth. I shall use you in many ways you know not of. I shall use you to light the fires of passion in the hearts of others. I have fashioned you with precision and care. And now, I send you forth to proclaim My heart of passion for My people!

I Love You, My Child!

Your Father

Truly, Father,

There is a passion in my heart that I desire to share with others. I will joyfully spend my life sharing Your heart of love and passion. Father, with Your help, I will be strong, brave, and bold, with gentleness, gratefulness, and love!

Loving Father, How can I share Your loving Presence today?

Amen

"For with God nothing will be impossible."
Luke 1:37 NKJV

My Beloved Child,

Stand straight and tall in My Spirit. Let your heart be strong in the knowledge of My love for you. You cried out, and I answered. You shall continue to prosper and grow in the light of My Spirit, in the light of My love for you. Behold, all things are new! The old has passed, forever gone, and behold, the new has sprung forth as the noonday sun. Rejoice, My child, and be glad. Many have longed to see this day come forth in their lives. Your day has come. Be filled with the blessings of My love for you. Break forth into the new day with song.

It Is A New Day, My Child,

Your Father

Loving Father,

I have such an excitement in my heart for what is to come. Truly Your joy is my strength. Whatever the future holds, I know You will be there with me, showing me the way!

I love You, Father, and treasure every moment spent in Your Presence!

Amen

"Behold, I make all things new."
Revelation 21:5 NKJV

Day 267

My Precious Child,

In the midst of the storm, I have kept you safe. I have poured My oil of gladness over you. Rest secure in My arms, secure from harm. With love, I encircle you. Have faith for My love will soothe and enfold you. I want you to know that My love will continually set you free. It has been the ride of a lifetime, but it's only begun. You will learn how to run, with an expectant heart. My peace you will finally know. It truly is a new day, complete in every way. Settle within your heart this day, that I will truly make a way to bring forth your hopes and dreams; they will seem to be bursting forth from the seams.

You Are Blessed, My Child,

Your Loving Father

Loving Father,

My Father, Speak to my heart, for I am listening with anticipation!

You have cherished and loved me, protected, soothed, and enfolded me and taught me many truths to set my spirit free! I am excited about what is to come, for You will be there with me every step of the way. I love You, Father!

Amen

"But the Lord has become my High Tower and Defense, and my God the Rock of my refuge."
Psalm 94:22 AMP

Day 268

My Child,

Call to Me and I will answer. My rod (protection) and My staff (guidance), they comfort you. Straight and narrow is the path that leads to life everlasting. Faithfulness and trustworthiness is the key to walking uprightly before Me. Stand tall in My Presence. Be content in My Presence with the carefreeness of youth, knowing that nothing can touch you that has not been filtered through My love. Precious in My sight are those who release unto Me all anxiety and fear. Go forth with transforming joy and peace.

I Love You, My Child,

Your Father

Loving Father,

It is so freeing to know that nothing can touch me that has not been filtered through Your love! To know that no matter how hard and difficult the road, You are with me leading, guiding, and bringing forth precious fruit in my life. I can face my life with the carefreeness of youth, without anxiety and fear, with a song of praise and thanksgiving in my heart. I love You, Father!

Dear Father, Are there areas where the words of my mouth do not match the sound of Your voice?

Amen

"They called upon the Lord, and He answered them."
Psalm 99:6 AMP

My Child,

I have swept, made clean, and have established you on high ground, removed from the clamor and din of lower roads, filled with the muck and mire of confusion. Stay on the high road that My Spirit creates within your heart, allowing you to rejoice in the completeness of My love and peace that brings forth My joy. Of My seasons, My times, and My ways, you are learning. This season will bring forth fruit and wisdom. Settle in for the duration and fear not, for your faithfulness shall be known and rewarded.

You Are Precious To Me!

Your Loving Father

Loving Father,

Father, I come to You today with a listening ear!

Thank You for the giftings, anointings, and callings that You have placed upon my life. How exciting to know that You are cultivating me and providing for my life's journey. Thank You, Father, for the gift of faithfulness, peace, and steadfastness!

Amen

"The Lord will establish you as a people holy to Himself,"
Deuteronomy 28:9 AMP

Day 270

My Precious Child,

When life has been hard, I have held your hand and together we have walked through the darkness. I have held you steady and created within your heart a trust and strength. You have seen the light of My smile upon you. My light has overcome the dark places in your life and overcome the heaviness of your soul. I rejoice with you, as you step forth each day in total reliance on Me and confidence in My steadfast love.

Bask In The Light Of My Smile,

Your Loving Father

Precious Father,

Truly You bring comfort and strength to my heart. You have held my hand and kept me steady as we've walked through the darkness together, causing me to trust You with my whole heart because of Your constant and loving Presence! You are my song!

Father, Thank You for Your faithfulness and steadfast love to me!

Amen

"Even the darkness hides nothing from You, but the night shines as the day; the darkness and the light are both alike to You."
Psalm 139:12 AMP

My Precious Child,

I have held you in My arms, bringing comfort to your wearied soul. I have loved you with an everlasting love and now, together, we shall see the weary restored, the prisoner set free, and the lost found. You have counted the cost, fought the good fight, and shouted the victory to a stagnant world. You shall comfort them as I have comforted you, pointing them to Me, and I shall lift their burden and set them free.

Comfort My People!

Your Loving Father

Precious Father,

Father, Who would You have me reach out to this day?

I am so thankful for Your care in my life. You have taught me gently and tenderly. Help me to be a living example, leading others to You. Thank You that I can come to You any minute of any day and soak in Your comfort and listen to Your Words of love and encouragement. I come to You now.

Amen

"Who comforts us in all our tribulation, that we may be able to comfort those who are in any trouble, with the comfort with which we ourselves are comforted by God."

2 Corinthians 1:4 NKJV

Day 272

My Child,

Each day is like a treasure handed to you untouched by human hands, divine and holy. Value each day as a special gift, charted and designed from the foundation of the earth. My blessed ones hear My voice and are satisfied. They know My heart of love toward them and walk unafraid. Stand strong and fearlessly in the confidence of My love and protection, for many are the challenges, but My hand sustains and protects you and causes you to flourish and grow. Stand guard against the enemy and shout for joy! Walk hand in hand with Me. My Spirit proclaims victory over your life. Be refreshed this day.

You Are Blessed, My Child!

Your Loving Father

Loving Father,

More and more I am seeing the miracle of each day that You have created for me! Each day help me to see the delights and blessings. Father, help me to wake each morning with a song in my heart for You!

Father, I bring these challenges to You for wisdom and understanding:

Amen

"This is the day the LORD has made;
We will rejoice and be glad in it."
Psalm 118:24 NKJV

My Child,

It is My delight to fill your life with happiness. The seasons of your life are changing. Joy is yours. My Word, you have treasured. My songs have been in your heart. My beauty has made your heart sing, and My love has held you strong. A new day is coming and it will be said, "There is music and laughter in your voice," but there shall be laughter and a new joy in your soul also! These are My special gifts to you. Come to the well and drink deeply, My child, that your life might overflow with joy. Your laughter shall be, full and free. Tremendous things lie ahead, ready to be explored and enjoyed.

Come Laugh With Me, My Child,

Your Loving Father

Loving Father,

Thank You, Father, that walking with You is such an adventure!

You have come in the silence and turned the silence to gold with Your Presence! Truly, Your beauty has made my heart sing, and Your love has held me strong. Already there is a new joy in my soul. There is such excitement in my heart for the things that lie ahead. Thank You, Father, for filling my life with laughter and joy. I love You, Father!

Amen

"He will yet fill your mouth with laughter [Job] and your lips with joyful shouting."
Job 8:21 AMP

Precious One,

Seek Me. I am the Creator of all. Circumstances shall not derail what I have created for you. Tattered and torn may be the many plans of those around you, but I am your anchor. Keep your focus on Me, and you will always land on your feet. Be fortified by My Word to your heart, which is constantly available to you. Sing, confidently, in the face of the enemy. Stand amazed at what I shall do with, for, and through you, for My Presence and glory sustains, leads, guides, and comforts you, and will be the strong tower on which you stand and have your being.

I Am Always With You!

Your Loving Father

Father,

Thank You for always helping me to keep my focus on You, not on what is happening around me, so that I can always land on my feet and continue on the path You have predestined for me. Father, teach me to trust You in all things!

Loving Father, My focus is on You today.

Amen

*"My mercy and loving-kindness will I keep
for him forevermore, and My covenant shall
stand fast and be faithful with him."
Psalm 89:28 AMP*

My Precious One,

Precious are My children who sit at My knee to receive. They are secure. They know they are protected and that nothing can harm them. They play and explore, but always within the boundaries they know will please and bring joy to their Father. Then, back they come to His knee, to bask in and share His love and His pleasure in them. You have always been this child in whom I could take joy and pride. Moment-by-moment, hearing My Word, much learning has taken place at My knee. All that I have is yours.

I Take Joy In You, My Child,

Your Loving Father

Thank You, Father,

Loving Father, My heart is open, ready to hear Your Words of direction!

That when I get weary and need to be refreshed, I can always come back to Your Presence, any time of the day or night, and share Your love. I desire to draw on Your wisdom, knowledge, peace, and joy — for You will always be my beloved Heavenly Father.

Amen

"Since you are precious in My sight,
You have been honored, and I have loved you;"
Isaiah 43:4 NKJV

Day 276

My Child,

I've chosen for you a higher way—to be a blessing each day in all that you say. Avoid every confusion and dissolution—disguised as concern for the flock. My heart has always been for you, to put your heart in all that you do. Reflect My love each and every day. Fulfill the call upon your life, and don't hold back. Blossom in My soft, gentle rain. Be confident, but walk humbly and receive My every blessing.

I Love You!

Your Loving Father

Loving Father,

Teach me daily to pursue the dreams You have placed in my heart. Help me to look to You when all about my life seems uncertain. Teach me to walk in confidence of Your love, yet humbly, to fulfill the call upon my life.

Father, Help me walk out my life each day as You would desire.

Amen

"Those who know your name will trust in you, for you, LORD, have never forsaken those who seek you."
Psalm 9:10 NIV

My Child,

Fear not the darkness, for I am shining brightly to bring you through into My glorious light. I have great compassion for you. My love for you is tremendous and I long to spend each day with you. Come forth into the healing of My Presence. Call to Me and seek Me out and watch My blessing fall upon you. The heaviness will lift, and My glory shall surround your life with freshness, renewal, and the joy of My Spirit.

I Hold You Close To My Heart!

Your Loving Father

Precious Father,

Loving Father, Shine Your light upon my life today.

Thank You that You never leave me or forsake me, and that You are always near to comfort me. Thank You for Your promises that give hope, understanding, and melt my heart with compassion. Thank You for Your devotion in my life. I love You, Father!

Amen

"The Lord is near to all who call upon Him,
to all who call upon Him sincerely and in truth."
Psalm 145:18 AMP

My Child,

Do you not know that I am ever watchful over you? Don't be anxious over your life, but stand still, intently with perseverance of spirit. Lift your heart to Me and rejoice, knowing that My guiding and protecting hand is near. I am your Salvation. I am fighting for you, and ours is the victory!

I Am With You Always!

Your Loving Father

Loving Father,

I choose to trust You — rejoicing in You, knowing that ours is always the victory. Help me to remember to allow You the freedom to bring about Your plans for my life, in Your way and in Your perfect timing. That is how I desire to live, Father, with Your help.

Father, Are there areas in my life that I am trying to handle myself, without Your guidance?

Amen

"Do not be seized with alarm and struck with fear, little flock, for it is your Father's good pleasure to give you the kingdom!"
Luke 12:32 AMP

My Precious Child,

Now, lay down your life before Me. My Words and compassion are guiding your way. My wisdom and knowledge are yours for the asking. You shall hear with My ears and see with My eyes, and your feet shall go where I lead you to go. I shall enlarge your sphere of influence for I have planned great things for you. You are My delight. Be lifted up and confident of this very thing, that I have begun a good work in your life and will complete it.

My Heart Rejoices Over You!

Your Loving Father

Beloved Father,

Thank You that You are bringing the desires of my heart to pass beyond what I could ask or think! You are my life, Father!

Amen

Loving Father, My heart sings a song to You of love and deep gratefulness!

"Being confident of this very thing, that He who has begun a good work in you will complete it"
Philippians 1:6 NKJV

My Child,

My Spirit descends as a dove and rests gently and lightly upon those who profess My Name. It rests as joy immeasurable. It rests as a protective shield. Be a confident runner in My race, knowing My umbrella of protection follows over you. As long as you are running in My race, you will not run out from under My protection. Confidence in Me is the key, assurance that I will never let you down. Run with courage, persistence, singleness of mind, and a continual focus on Me.

Be Confident In My Love,

Your Loving Father

Faithful Father,

Your Words of encouragement and love bring courage and confidence to my heart! Help me to avoid reverting back to my old ways of responding with fear and frustration. I know as long as I keep my focus on You that my life will have meaning and purpose. Thank You for Your constant protection and care.

Loving Father, My heart is listening for Your Words of life.

Amen

"And the Lord said, My Presence shall go with you, and I will give you rest."
Exodus 33:14 AMP

My Child,

You have longed for carefree days of play. Your days of sunshine and hope are here. You have been faithful and ever patient. Sing My praises for I bring renewal to your life and refreshing to your heart. Hope has come alive in your spirit and the future shines brightly. Days of joyful activity are approaching! Go forth now with a song in your heart, refreshed and revived.

Sing With Me, My Child!

Your Loving Father

Beloved Father,

Father, Thank You for new days of joy and hope.

You always bring good things to my life. You have strengthened and prepared me with Your power and Your Word. Thank You, Father, for training me and lovingly teaching me to hear Your voice in my heart! Thank You for filling my heart with hope, once again.

Amen

"Sing to the Lord a new song, and His praise from the end of the earth!"
Isaiah 42:10 AMP

My Child,

There shall come upon you a new radiance from above. It shall shine like the morning sun. My ways will become more and more your ways, and you shall know the peace, joy, and contentment of the Salvation of your Lord. Unto those who heed My voice, the reward is great. Cast all of your cares upon Me, for I love you. I am your burden bearer. Many are the trials of this world, but you shall safely move through them, knowing I am your strength and your shield. Strength and confidence comes through encounter, and faith is renewed through battles won. Rejoice, and be mightily glad, for ours is the victory, always!

My Treasures Await You,

Your Faithful Father!

My Faithful Father,

Every Word that You speak amplifies a promise You have already spoken to the world! Security with You lasts forever. Help me to rest in Your arms of love and security. I want to hear Your voice clearly. Situations come and go, but this is my solid goal; to walk with You in such a way, as to never miss a single Word spoken by You.

Father, I want to hear Your Words to my heart.

Amen

"They go from strength to strength [increasing in victorious power];"
Psalm 84:7 AMP

Day 283

My Child,

March on victoriously, knowing that in Me, the battle has been won, and the reward shall be great. Do not be afraid of challenges. Rejoice knowing that I am there to walk you through to triumph. Keep your eyes on Me, and walk through the land as I guide. Each encounter is an incredible discovery. The struggle is Mine. Give it all to Me. Be steadfast!

Do Not Give Up!

Your Faithful Father

Loving Father,

My Father, Teach my heart to hear Your voice—I don't want to miss a single Word!

You have been so faithful in my life. When I look back, I can see that each battle won has brought tremendous reward into my life. You have made me stronger and more resilient. But most important, every victory won has taught me to love and trust You more. I love You, Father!

Amen

"Blessed (happy, to be envied) is the man who is patient under trial and stands up under temptation, for when he has stood the test and been approved, he will receive [the victors] crown of life which God promised to those who love Him."
James 1:12 AMP

My Beloved Child,

My peace that passes all understanding is yours today. You have entered through the door of understanding into the workings of My Spirit. Be strong. I am by your side to strengthen and sustain your spirit. I am faithful and will be diligent to carry you through to victory. Be confident in Me. Reach out for your victory.

I Love You, My Child,

Your Father

Precious Father,

Thank You for Your awesome, guiding hand on my life. You have been so faithful and diligent, carrying me through to victory. How wonderful to know that You are strengthening me each day and creating for me all that You have preordained for my life. I do trust You, Lord, with all of my heart.

Loving Father, What am I holding back that is keeping me from trusting You fully?

Amen

"He shall not be afraid of evil tidings;
his heart is firmly fixed, trusting
(leaning on and being confident) in the Lord."
Psalm 112:7 AMP

My Child,

Run the good race. Finish the course with honor. Persistence and determination will keep you striving onward. Keep your eyes ever looking upward to Christ. Persist! Prayer, thanksgiving, and praise will propel you forward. Remain steadfast on your course. Don't let yourself get distracted. Run the good race. It will take uprightness, stamina, fitness, purity, determination, perseverance, and strength. Most of all, remember that I am by your side all the way.

I Am Always With You,

Your Loving Father

Father,

I am looking to You for strength. Help me to press ever onward and continue on to the victory. Help me to remain steadfast and sure in the knowledge that You are running with me and securing the victory!

Loving Father, Thank You for helping me finish this course in my life with honor.

Amen

"*Let us run with patient endurance and steady and active persistence the appointed course of the race that is set before us.*"
Hebrews 12:1 AMP

My Child,

Don't be troubled for I have all things in My hand. All the details of your life are known to Me. Dwell in the shadow of My wing. I will never forsake you. When adversity comes, rest and trust in My strength. I will replace sorrow with happiness and renewal. Don't look back at the trials of yesterday. Always look upward and onward.

You Are Blessed, My Child,

Your Loving Father

Loving Father,

It is so comforting to know that nothing takes You by surprise, that I can always trust and rely on You! Even in the midst of hardship I am able to come to You and receive Your steadfast and loving comfort. Let each day pass as You have ordained. Help me let go of the concerns that burden my heart and rest in the protection of Your awesome love.

Father, This day brings with it the choice to enter into it with absolute trust in Your hand upon my life.

Amen

"Keep and guard me as the pupil of Your eye;
hide me in the shadow of Your wings."
Psalm 17:8 AMP

My Child,

Rejoice for the work that is taking place in your life, for the restoration that I am working in your spirit. Be not afraid of your own thoughts, for you are taking on My thoughts within you. I am restoring your joy, peace, trust, and faith in a new and more expanded way. I am building your life spiritually, stone-on-stone, with a strength that cannot be toppled. Each stone bears My Name, and within it, My perfection and completeness. So wrestle not with the uncertainty that you feel, but take comfort in the knowledge that each invested stone is being placed one by one as I would have it.

I Am With You!

You Loving Father

Loving Father,

Precious Father, I'm listening for Your Words to me.

You bring such happiness to my heart. Your Presence delights my soul, and Your love sets me free in ways I never dreamed I would be! You constantly bring renewal for me to enjoy along this road called life! I am so grateful, Father! Nothing can compare with the great joy that comes from realizing it is You speaking with great love and wisdom to my heart.

Amen

"In the multitude of my [anxious] thoughts within me,
Your comforts cheer and delight my soul!"
Psalm 94:19 AMP

My Child,

Your life is in transformation. Do not expect the new to be as the old. Expect a new and perfect thing in your life constantly. You are My beloved child. Extend your faith and trust that I have a design for your life. Look up and rejoice and know that I am the Lord of all. Don't be afraid when the waves of life crash all around you, for you will find sure footing all along your pathway. Know that each time you place your step, just as each time you take a breath, you will find your ultimate destination smoothly. March out, one step at a time, knowing that each slide is as a stone being laid upon the foundation of My Kingdom within you, which cannot be shaken.

Be My Tenacious Child,

Your Father

Loving Father,

Daily walking in trust with You is exciting, and knowing that each step is secure in You makes it an adventure. It is so comforting to know that You see the end from the beginning and have everything that pertains to my life held safely in Your hands of love! Every day is a gift from You, loving Father. I love You!

Father, What new things do You have to share with me today?

Amen

"Teach me, O LORD, to follow every one of your principles."
Psalm 119:33 NLT

My Child,

Think of life as a classroom with much to be learned. Don't discard the seemingly insignificant parts, for what seems small can many times be the key component. Take each day in stride, as allotted, with praise and thanksgiving. Seek My wisdom. Look for the open doors of opportunity. There are no vacuums or empty spaces in My Kingdom. All things work together to form the whole. Be at peace and receive from Me.

You Are Doing Well!

Your Loving Father

Loving Father,

Father, Teach me, I pray, to be more aware of Your moment-by-moment Presence with me!

There is such peace in knowing that life is a continuous learning process all combined together to make the whole. I want to relax in Your Spirit and refrain from much ado over nothing. Help me to completely rely on You for every breath I take—every decision, every thought. I want to be more aware, moment-by-moment of Your Presence.

Amen

"For whoever finds me [Wisdom] finds life and draws forth and obtains favor from the Lord."
Proverbs 8:35 AMP

Day 290

My Precious One,

Happy is the one who trusts in and truly relies on My leadings, for he shall feast at My table of blessing each morning and be at peace. Allay your self-styled worries and anxieties. Trust in My guiding and protecting hand. Let Me bring things about, and do not fret in the meantime. Stand tall in My Spirit. Partake of My banquet table, for it has been set for you. Grow in My love for you daily and faithfully.

I Love You,

Your Father

Loving Father,

Basic trust! It all boils down to basic trust. I want to trust You in all things. I want to be at peace in all things. Help me, Father, to always remember to be as Your little lamb, perfectly trusting in Your guiding and protective hand, starting each day peacefully feeding on the dew laid and tender grasses, and being at peace the rest of the day.

Father, Once again, I give You my worries and anxieties so that I can walk peacefully with You and follow Your leading.

Amen

"I have set the Lord continually before me; because He is at my right hand, I shall not be moved."
Psalm 16:8 AMP

When God Speaks to My Heart

My Child,

Eliminate hurt, fear, and all negatives. Replace them with love and faithfulness. Speak life. Be a proclaimer of My peace. Establish My love. You are surrounded by My angels; you shall go forth unafraid. Let go of the overwhelming forces of frustration and rejection, and look to Me for your worth and abundance. I shall carry you forth with ease and simplicity, and it shall be known, to My glory, that all is well with your soul, for I have established it so. My love overshadows, protects, and carries you forth into uncharted territory. Strong, immovable, and filled with My power are those who stand in My grace and proclaim the awesome and sustaining power of their God!

You Are Precious To Me,

Your Loving Father

Father,

Loving Father, All is well with my soul as I stay in Your Presence, always listening for Your direction and Words of life!

Life is so pure and simple when I remember to speak life — Your Word — and look to You for my worth and abundance. Whenever I let the negatives creep in, life becomes complicated. Help me to walk in the positive. Thank You, Father, for teaching me always to live and speak with an optimistic heart.

Amen

"To the end that my tongue and my
heart and everything glorious within me
may sing praise to You and not be silent.
O Lord my God, I will give thanks to You forever."
Psalm 30:12 AMP

Day 292

My Child,

From the crown of your head to the soles of your feet shall My Spirit be with you, abide with you, and rest upon you. Enter into each day with expectancy in the ability to see Me in every event. Seek to be faithful, standing in love, even when you stare in the face of the unloving. Be content in life. Destiny fulfilled is the greatest joy, for it brings together contentness and wisdom—all the gifts of My Spirit brought together by living in My Presence.

My Favor Is Upon You,

Your Loving Father

Loving Father,

Living in Your Presence is the joy of my life and the reason for my life! Your wonder and beauty are everywhere I look. Precious Father, Your love permeates all of creation! Daily I see destiny fulfilled in my life and in the lives of others. Precious Lord, I love You!

Beloved Father, How can I honor You today?

Amen

"Blessed be the Lord! For he has shown me
His marvelous loving favor."
Psalm 31:21 AMP

My Child,

Fortify your stand of faith by spending time in My Presence. You are among My greatest treasures. Rejoice at the gentle sound of My voice. Together we shall walk, talk, sing, and enjoy the blessings each day brings. For within each day, My will is fulfilled in your life. Be blessed with My very best offerings. Go forward now, unafraid and knowing full well that I, your God, your faithful friend, know the beginning from the end.

You Are My Treasure!

Your Loving Father

Dear Father,

My faithful friend, I love walking, talking, and enjoying the blessings of each day with You. Truly each day is filled with Your abundance, whether through the smile of a "Heart Friend," the music of shared laughter, or a surprise from Your heart. Thank You for your blessings upon my life.

Precious Father, To hear Your voice is always the choice of my heart!

Amen

"My beloved is mine and I am his!"
Song of Solomon 2:16 AMP

My Child,

Remember I am ever watchful over you—ever near. There are times and seasons. Winter is the time of seclusion and rest, reflection, healing, preparation, and stretching. Spring brings expanded vision, clearing from the storms, renewed hope, and new vision. Summer is implementation and the joy of fulfillment. Autumn is change and the seeking of new paths. Each season brings its own challenges. Cling to Me in every thought, word, and action. Rejoice in each season.

I Am With You Always,

Your Loving Father

Loving Father,

Thank You for the beauty, blessing, and revelation of each season in my life. Help me to remember to stand straight and tall, with my back to the wind—all the while looking to You. Help me finish the course with steadfast determination. Strengthen me as I seek you. Your Word is like a rock to me that cannot be moved or swayed. With You, Father, the best is yet to come!

Father, What would have me learn from Your Word today?

Amen

"I will bless the Lord at all times; His praise
shall continually be in my mouth."
Psalm 34:1 AMP

My Precious Child,

It is My peace that sustains you and makes your life worthwhile. It is a treasure more precious than silver or gold, and must be maintained at all times, at all cost. When the flame of peace flickers, sit in My Presence. Peace is, and always has been, the barometer of My life within you. As you seek My heart, you shall become a transmitter of My peace and love. Continue on, My child, with blessing surrounding you. It is My favor that opens doors and My peace and love that will allow you to go through those doors, bringing fulfillment and joy.

I Am Your Peace, My Child,

Your Loving Father

Loving Father,

Beloved Father, Here I am, seeking Your peace in a greater way than I have known before.

Your favor truly surrounds me with Your peace and love. When in doubt, help me to remember to follow Your heart, for truly Your Presence is the restoration of life within me. Your peace sustains me and makes life worthwhile. It is a treasure more precious than anything I have ever known.

Amen

"For He is [Himself] our peace (our bond of unity and harmony)."
Ephesians 2:14 AMP

My Precious One,

Be fearless and live courageously. The measure of a person is the ability to love, and stand in faithfulness and truth. Look to My guiding and sustaining Spirit to empower your heart. Invite Me into every area of your life and let Me bring you joy. Hope is My gift to you. Bask in the glory of My love so that My blessings will continue to be poured out upon you without measure. Praise paves the way to success as you walk in My Spirit, which is love.

You Are Precious To Me,

Your Loving Father

Loving Father,

Hope is the gift that You have given to me, and it is such joy to walk and live out my life with such purpose and meaning. Each day is a new gift from You—a treasure. I love and trust You, Father. Thank You for Your guiding hand upon my life, my family, and all those I love. You are awesome!

Beloved Father, Here I am in Your Presence.

Amen

*"Since we have such [glorious] hope
(such joyful and confident expectation),
we speak very freely and openly and fearlessly."*
2 Corinthians 3:12 AMP

My Precious Child,

It brings Me great pleasure to see My children at harmony with one another. Share with those I have placed in your life — My great love. Let them know that My heart reaches out to them. Lift Me up with joy and show others the way to My heart. The way of hope, faithfulness, and the ability to stand unmoved by the world and outside pressures, by taking in My Word. Stand steady, My child, and faint not, but see Me in the midst of all things. Start now to rejoice, for victory in your life begins now, and you shall experience great triumph in your God as you take pleasure in Me.

I Take Pleasure In You, My Child,

Your Loving Father

Wonderful Father,

Thank You for teaching me to stand, unmoved by the world and outside pressures, by hearing Your Word, staying in Your Presence, and seeing You in the midst of all things. It has been a long, long road, but one in which You have been faithful to me, and now I can readily see the victory in every struggle and trial.

Loving Father, My heart is listening with loving anticipation!

Amen

"Let love for your fellow believers continue and be a fixed practice with you [never let it fail]."
Hebrews 13:1 AMP

Day 298

My Child,

Shower your love on others with no fear of lack of return, for I return in abundance and refill your reservoir to overflowing. In the past, you have looked to others for that restoration. Only I have the power to restore. Look to Me, and give as I lead and as My Word directs. See your reward in Me, not in others. I will reward you openly and without reservation. Go forward this day with the assurance that you can never be hurt again, for your reward does not come from people; your reward comes from Me. Continue to see Me as your provider in all things. Together, we shall walk new ground and see new vistas of splendor, for more is available when you look only to Me as your source. Let us proceed.

I Love You,

Your Father

Loving Father,

Thank You, for being my provider in all things. Only You have the power to refill. Thank You, Father, for helping me keep my outlook and hopes toward You and not on others. You are the Creator of the universe. You are my source! Help me to love others fully, without expectations, loving simply for love's sake, because You are their source, too!

Wonderful Father, Who can I reach out to and befriend today?

Amen

"He who sows righteousness (moral and spiritual rectitude in every area and relation) shall have a sure reward [permanent and satisfying]."
Proverbs 11:18 AMP

When God Speaks to My Heart

My Precious Child,

My hand is upon your life. Don't give in, but rather press on. Be not afraid of the slow start. Rest in My preparations and My love for you. Step-by-step, day-by-day, resolve to walk in what I have given you to walk in, and more will be added. Let go of the pressure and don't allow yourself to be frustrated over what seems to be lack of action. It is there. Remain in My peace for you. Do not let oppression knock on your door, for all shall go as I have planned. Remain unmoved by outside stresses. Simply move as I lead, step-by-step. Remain agile and alert. Be at peace, My child.

All Is In My Loving Care,

Your Father

Beloved Father,

Loving Father, My heart reaches out to You for strength and wisdom.

It is so comforting to know that You have a plan for my life. I can simply remain steadfast and move as You lead, step-by-step. It is the continual pressing in that builds the strong foundation. I can simply resolve to walk in Your strength and rely on Your power to move on my behalf. Father, help me to always remain agile and alert and at peace! I love You, Father!

Amen

"The Lord preserves all those who love Him,"
Psalm 145:20 AMP

My Child,

Wave from afar as you traverse this road, intent upon the fulfillment of My Word to you. Wave from afar to the demands upon your time, that would steal away your moments with Me. Wave from afar to the negative advice, to defeat, and dismay, for unto you I give the gifts of straightforward trust, faith, and understanding. Doubt and gloom cannot touch you. Blessings and fulfillment are your portion. They are My gifts to you.

I Love You, My Child,

Your Father

Beloved Father,

It brings my heart great peace just thinking of You. You give such wonderful blessings. Your promises build my trust, faith, understanding, and happiness beyond measure. How wonderful to simply turn my back to defeat, dismay, doubt, and the demands that would try to steal away my relationship with You. I love You, Father!

Loving Father, I am intent on what You have to share with me today!

Amen

"And whatever you ask for in prayer, having faith and [really] believing, you will receive."
Matthew 21:22 AMP

My Child,

I raise a standard before you to walk in. Walk in My ways unflinchingly. Cry aloud saying, "My God is an awesome God. Nothing is too difficult for Him!" You will find within your heart a new openness to respond with love—free to receive without restraint. Laughter comes with freedom. Be free! Stand aside and watch Me work. Say not to yourself, "The weight is too heavy," instead say, "My God is faithful." Go forth this day with a song in your heart and a bounce in your step, for My faithfulness is your life.

Be Free, My Child, Be Free!

Your Loving Father

My Faithful Father,

Father, Here I am, in Your Presence, listening with all my heart!

Forgive me for the times when I am tempted to take on the burdens of life. Your faithfulness is my life and my song! What joy, to be able to stand aside and watch You work, bringing such wonderful things to pass, things that cause my heart to sing! Laughter is such a wonderful gift from You! No wonder it is such a precious gift.

Amen

"God is faithful (reliable, trustworthy, and therefore ever true to His promise, and He can be depended on);"
1 Corinthians 1:9 AMP

My Child,

Walk in your life—freely. Live a life of abundance. Stand back, survey, and forgive. It is a testament of My Spirit residing and acting in you. Daily cleanse your heart of all the built-up debris. Don't allow the day, to pile up, surround, and overpower you. Discard it all. Go forth this day, determined to be My clear channel of love, free from all bondages. Lay down your life before Me. Minister life to those around you! Build up their hearts, and they shall see the glory of their God. Walk in My goodness, live freely, and be unencumbered.

You Are Precious To Me!

Your Loving Father

Loving Father,

I want to live freely and unencumbered. Help me to walk in forgiveness. Father, I am determined to be a clear channel of Your love, free from the bondages of unforgiveness. Please help me to remember to build up others' hearts, and minister life to those around me. I love You, Father!

Father, Forgive me for negative words spoken. Cleanse my heart, I pray. Help me to always speak positive, uplifting, and encouraging words.

Amen

"Judge not, and you shall not be judged.
Condemn not, and you shall not be condemned.
Forgive, and you will be forgiven."
Luke 6:37 NKJV

My Child,

Live your life with confidence, don't allow yourself to be held back. Victory comes in stages, like climbing stairs. Don't be fainthearted, but press straight ahead undaunted by the passing scene. Learn as you spend time with Me. Triumphant and glorious are the days ahead, filled with the glory of My love. Walls will be restored that were once broken down. Restoration is ahead by My hand of love. Continue on in undaunted faith and in the truth of My love—for an abundant life awaits you.

I Love You, My Child,

Your Father

Beloved Father,

Loving Father, Thank You for speaking to my heart with such love and acceptance!

It is so exciting to see Your unconditional love, acceptance, and healing in my life. Father, every day walking with You is an adventure and a joy. At the same time, there has been such a visible progression of restoration in my life by Your hand of love. Father, thank You for establishing my faith deeply in Your unconditional love!

Amen

"For we walk by faith…not by sight or appearance."
2 Corinthians 5:7 AMP

My Child,

Walk uprightly and sure-footed. Conquer the challenges that lie ahead and hold fast to the promises I have given you. Don't struggle with inconsistencies of life. Let Me do the choreography as I lead. You will not miss out on My best, and I will not allow your foot to stumble. Straight are the pathways laid out by Me. Be at peace and watch the scenario unfold. You will see wonders beyond imagination, and My Spirit shall rejoice over you.

I Direct Your Steps!

Your Loving Father

Loving Father,

Thank You that no matter what is going on around me, I can trust You! Thank You for not allowing my foot to stumble. Truly, You have taught me that You will fulfill Your promises to me. That knowledge brings such peace to my heart!

My Father, Guide my steps today.

Amen

"When you walk, your steps shall not be hampered [your path will be clear and opened]; and when you run, you shall not stumble."
Proverbs 4:12 AMP

My Child,

I am leading your way and will continue. Laid out before you is My plan for your life. Don't be afraid or reluctant to go forward in areas of concern. I am watching over you. Don't worry because much of your life seems filled with questions and concerns, for My hand is upon you, and My love for you is constant and true. My design for your life is full of goodness and peace. Know that I have created for you, a panorama of blessing and purpose in your life, to bring forth My will in all its fullness.

You Are Precious To Me, My Child,

Your Loving Father

Beloved Father,

Father, Thank You for Your love, which is constant and true!

Thank You for continuing, each and everyday, to guide and lead my life. I lift my faith and heart to You knowing You will bring blessing and purpose to my life. One thing I know, You love me, and I can trust You in every area of my life and in the lives of those I love!

Amen

"The precepts of the Lord are right, rejoicing the heart; the commandment of the Lord is pure and bright, enlightening the eyes."
Psalm 19:8 AMP

My Beloved Child,

You are covered by the strength of My protection. My heart's desire is shown forth in the magnitude of My love and support toward you. My protection and love bring joy and happiness to each new day. Release the heaviness that has built up. Release unto Me all the byproducts of those burdens, weariness, trials, tribulations, joylessness, sorrow, and despair. Sense My Presence, My child, and know My power. Come through the gates of My Presence singing and into My courts with praise. Serve Me with gladness, thanksgiving, and lightness of heart. Take into your heart peace and joy. Look to Me in trust, love, praise, and with the fullness of joy.

I Will Never Forsake You!

Your Loving Father

I love You, my Father!

You speak to me with such gentle love and care! I release unto You the heaviness that has built up, especially the weariness of heart, choosing instead the strength of Your protection and the magnitude of Your love and support toward me!

Loving Father, Thank You for speaking to my heart, and for being my source of joy, gladness, and peace!

Amen

"Cast your burden on the Lord [releasing
the weight of it] and He will sustain you;
He will never allow the [consistently] righteous
to be moved (made to slip, fall, or fail)."
Psalm 55:22 AMP

My Precious One,

I love you! A deeper knowing of this is yours this day. It is a gift given. Open your heart to receive it with thanksgiving. My love is unconditional. It is constant. It is filled with grace. Starting today, you shall more fully know the preciousness of My love, our hearts beating as one. Listen with tenacity. Listen with strength of purpose. Listen with faith to receive. Listen and believe!

Receive My Gift Of Love!

Your Loving Father

Loving Father,

Father, Thank You for Your gift of love!

Everywhere I look, there You are! Your love surrounds me with beauty. Thank You, Father, that today I can more fully know the preciousness of Your love. I want to think Your thoughts, and listen always with strength of purpose and with the faith to receive everything You say to my heart. I love You, Father!

Amen

*"God is love, and he who abides in love
abides in God, and God in him."*
1 John 4:16 NKJV

My Child,

Revel in the completeness of all I have created for you to experience, that you might proclaim My faithfulness. I have been with you every step of your life. Trust in Me. Rest in My care and know My loving hand is upon you. Faithfulness is the key; My faithfulness to you and your faithfulness to Me. Rejoice in the quiet days of reflection. Rejoice in the hectic days knowing My protection is over you. Rejoice in the days of shared love. They are all by My hand.

I Am Always With You,

Your Loving Father

Loving Father,

Every step that I take You have prepared ahead for me. Build up in me confidence and assurance in Your guiding hand. Thank You, Father, for the completeness of all You have created for me to experience, that I might proclaim Your faithfulness in my life. Father, Thank You, for always being there.

Amen

"Now the just shall live by faith."
Hebrews 10:38 NKJV

My Precious Child,

During your life, you have learned to trust in Me. Within your heart beats the rhythm of My heart, a steady beat that only grace can give. You have depended on My grace to carry you through and thus extend that grace to others, knowing that grace can turn failure into success and sorrow into joy. My grace has been sufficient for you and shall continue to uphold you and make a way for you. My hand covers and protects you and gives you life and stability. Be at peace and rejoice with contentment and confidence in the outcome. Continue in confidence, as My hand of deliverance works in your life.

I Love You!

Your Faithful Father

Precious Father,

Father, Thank You for love.

What an awesome God You have been to me, through the many years that we have walked together! My heart rejoices and is satisfied. Please continue to lead my life—in all things. Thank You, Father, for Your faithfulness and love!

Amen

"And now abide faith, hope, love, these three;
but the greatest of these is love."
1 Corinthians 13:13 NKJV

Day 310

My Child,

Through the years, My Spirit has lifted you up and shown you a marvelous way of contentment and peace. I have blessed you in all of your ways. Through the years, My Spirit has comforted and lifted you. My Spirit has caused you to see that no matter what the circumstance, My love for you will always be the source of your strength, full and free. Believe this. Never doubt the power of My love and direction in your life.

You Are Precious To Me, My Child

Your Loving Father

Loving Father,

Thank You for the confidence You give! Your Spirit has caused me to see that no matter what the circumstance, Your love will always be the source of my strength and direction for my life. Help me keep my focus on the road You have mapped out for me. Thank You, Father, for Your faithful guidance and direction in my life. I love You!

Father, Speak to my heart.

Amen

"*Have faith in God [constantly].*"
Mark 11:22 AMP

My Beloved Child,

Your life has been fashioned by My hand. You are My handiwork. Be at peace, My child, as I fashion your life complete in every way. The ravages of time shall not harm you. Fear not the passing of time. Time is your friend, as I work within your life and a gift to be enjoyed. You are My treasure, transformed and changed into My image. Rejoice and be glad for My Spirit of truth is coming forth in your life. Fear not, for each moment of each day is protected by My hand.

You Are My Treasure!

Your Loving Father

Loving Father,

Father, I trust You.

Through the years Your Presence has been such a comfort to my heart. Please continued to fashion my life in Your image, complete in every way. You have blessed me with peace and contentment as I've taken refuge in You. I love You!

Amen

"The [uncompromisingly] righteous shall be glad in the Lord and shall trust and take refuge in Him;"
Psalm 64:10 AMP

My Child,

Stability and contentment go together to bring you to a place of fulfillment and confidence. In contentment and peace shall My promises come forth. The struggles have been great, but the reward shall be greater. Secure in My love you have been, able to see Me in every occurrence. Open up your heart and receive My love and abundant blessings.

I Am Forever With You, My Child,

Your Loving Father

Loving Father,

I love experiencing Your Presence in my life. You are so faithful, Father! I give to You all the struggles that have weighed me down, releasing them like dust in the wind. I love You, Father!

Father, Thank You for Your contentment and peace.

Amen

"Enlarge the place of your tent, and let the curtains of your habitation be stretched out;"
Isaiah 54:2 AMP

My Beloved Child,

Feast your eyes on the prize coming your way. Some are the desires of your heart resurrected; some the fulfillment of dreams past, and some the cry of your heart. You shall sit in amazement as you see the multitude of blessings coming your way. See the mystery of times past come into focus. See the answers to questions asked, revealed. Expectations shall be high, as you walk through this appointed time. Fluctuations, renovations, and revelation shall be the order of the day, as you draw ever closer to the fulfillment of My Words spoken.

You Have Been Faithful!

Your Father

Loving Father,

Father, Each day with You truly is a feast in Your Presence!

My expectations are high as I walk through this life with You. Help me stay along the path that You have mapped out for me to follow. Thank You, Father, for being with me, as I draw ever closer to the fulfillment of Your Words spoken.

Amen

"So run your race that you may lay hold of the prize"
1 Corinthians 9:24

My Precious One,

My strength has prevailed in your life and made you strong and resilient. Measure not physical strength with strength of character and strength of resolve. The heavens declare the victory of one who has walked the weary miles and prevailed. With a song in your heart and in your mouth you shall continue to march forth, with flags of celebration flowing in the wind. It shall be a walk of victory, not one of struggling to remain upright. Sincerity of heart has kept you on target. Now, the shout of victory shall lead you forth and cause your heart to burst forth with song and rejoicing.

I Am Proud Of You, My Child

Your Loving Father

Loving Father,

Help me to hear Your Words in my heart. I want Your Presence to shine out of my face and light the way before me. Guide me in all my ways. As a small child, hold my hand, as I walk through the unknown. Fill my life with the delight and the wonder of all new things. Father, I love You!

Father, Fill my life with hope and wonder as You speak to my heart!

Amen

"For whatever is born of God is victorious over the world; and this is the victory that conquers the world, even our faith."

1 John 5:4 AMP

Dear One,

It brings Me pleasure to bless you. Come to Me with your heart's desires and needs. I want to bless you. Receive from Me. Call out to Me and allow My hand to guide your life. Receive My Words through prayers and time with Me. My abundant life is yours. All that I have is yours, and you can receive life from Me and share it with those I have placed in your life. Receive and pass on! Receive and pass on!

You Are Precious To Me!

Your Loving Father

Loving Father,

Beloved Father, Thank You for Your covenant of love and life.

You have taught me that in order to walk in a covenant relationship with You or with others, I must walk in love, faithfulness, honor, trust, joy, and committed communication. Help me to stand firm in faith, believing You for the unbelievable, the impossible, and every dream of my heart. Thank You, Father, for every blessing in my life.

Amen

*"The Lord is near to all who call upon Him,
to all who call upon Him sincerely and in truth."*
Psalm 145:18 AMP

Day 316

My Child,

You have struggled long and hard to come into this place. I realize you still feel inadequate to the task, but all that you need is already within you. Your destiny is secure. Don't struggle to fulfill that destiny, but start each day with Me securely in the place of authority over your life. Take each day as it comes, rejoicing in Me. Be refreshed by Me. Refuse to be moved. When anxiety arises, let Me calm your inner being, moment-by-moment. Each day, step-by-step, move forward with confidence and peace in Me.

I Will Not Fail You!

Your Loving Father

Father, Thank You,

That I don't have to feel rushed and pressured; I can move forward toward the goal, with confidence and peace. Help me to remember that struggle is not necessary for success. I want to remain at peace in my life, and confident in Your ability to move on my behalf.

Father, Today I commit my way to You, confident that I shall prevail, for my adequacy is in You.

Amen

"Commit your way to the LORD, Trust also in Him, And He shall bring it to pass."
Psalm 37:5 NKJV

My Beloved Child,

Trust in Me and commit your way unto Me. I shall guide you each day. Be that standard-bearer of truth. Be open. Be established in My love. That is trust and forbearance; trust in My ability to work all for your good and forbearance to know I will protect you as you give out grace to others. You are to be a standard-bearer of forbearance and grace. It is by My hand that you shall stand and show forth My love and acceptance, total acceptance in humility and truth.

You Are Precious To Me!

Your Loving Father

Loving Father,

Father, I treasure this time with You.

Help me to walk in truth, patience, grace, humility, and loving acceptance, being established in Your love and trusting You to protect me, as You guide my life! Help me, Father, to simply walk in Your peace, straightforwardly with love! I love You, Father.

Amen

"O Lord of hosts, blessed (happy, fortunate, to be envied) is the man who trusts in You [leaning and believing on You, committing all and confidently looking to You, and that without fear or misgiving!]"
Psalm 84:12 AMP

Precious One,

Be as the eagle in flight and see as from above. Fly above the worries of the day. Be set free from concern and care. Fly high in the sky. Rely on My ability to provide for you. Be released and set free. Expand your vision. Open your eyes that you might see the mighty wonders I have for you. Many blessings await you. Take wing!

Fly Free, My Child, Fly Free!

Your Father

Loving Father,

I have a dream in my heart. Help me to keep my eyes on You. I want to fly like an eagle in flight with You, flying in freedom. I want to live my life carefree. I want to live with exuberance. I love You, Father!

Father, Speak to my heart.

Amen

"But those who wait on the LORD Shall renew
their strength; They shall mount up with wings
like eagles, They shall run and not be weary,
They shall walk and not faint."
Isaiah 40:31 NKJV

Precious One,

Let your heart sing all the day long, through the late-night hours, into the new dawn. Sing praise to Me, your Maker and Friend. Experience newfound peace within. My peace will come and turn the day of rain into sunshine. Be lifted up into higher realms of praise. Be set free from the pull downward. Fly high in the Heavenlies where the songs of angels are heard. Fly high in the sky. Fly above the problems and remain unruffled in My mantle of peace.

Sing With Me, My Precious One!

Your Father

Loving Father,

Father, My life is safely in Your hand.

Fill my heart with a song, that a smile would return to my face, laughter would ring from my voice, and peace would return to my life. Thank You, Father, for being faithful. I love You!

Amen

*"I will trust and not be afraid, for the
Lord God is my strength and song;"*
Isaiah 12:2 AMP

My Child,

Seasons of change have woven the tapestry of your life. But in each place, a touch of the Master's hand has molded and sustained you with love and the gift of grace. See My face of love and grace reflected in your life. Struggles cease with full release. You cannot fail for I am ever watchful over you. My love has made it so.

I Love You, My Child,

Your Father

Loving Father,

Your Presence in my life is so beautiful. It is so true that struggles cease when my heart remembers that I cannot fail, for Your love and grace have made it so. I can look at the tapestry of my life and see that You have caused each moment to be a gift of grace. I love You, Father!

Father, Your peace envelops me with such joy.

Amen

"…let me see your face, let me hear your voice; for your voice is sweet, and your face is lovely."
Song of Solomon 2:14 AMP

Day 321

My Precious Child,

Straight words of love, I speak; you have listened, blossomed, and flourished. The beauty is real and the fragrance is sweet to Me. The path you have taken has been no small feat. You have traveled the road with a trusting heart and listened intently. Seek My heart. Seek My restoration when you grieve. Lean into the gentle sound of My voice resounding clear. Hear Me saying "I love you," with clarity and grace. Receive My comforting Words of exhortation to heal your heart. See, hear, know, and sense My Presence.

I Am Ever Near,

Your Loving Father

Loving Father,

Father, Thank You for Your Words of love to my heart!

It is my desire to bear much fruit in my life. Thank You, Father, for helping me to continually hear Your loving voice with more clarity, that I would grow and flourish.

Amen

"When you bear (produce) much fruit,
My Father is honored and glorified,"
John 15:8 AMP

My Child,

My mercy has been here all along for you. Seek after My ways. Respect and love go hand in hand. Avoid strife and division. In My Presence, you can safely be vulnerable. Seek My heart, and you will see confusion leave. Strength of purpose standing strong, rejoice in My Presence. Seek the Giver of all things. Seek the peace My Presence brings.

Stay In My Peace!

Your Loving Father

Loving Father,

The wisdom and beauty of Your Words and Your heart set me free. Help me, Father, to remain humble, with respect and love. Your Presence brings healing to my heart and hope to my life. I am truly grateful.

Father, Thank You for the peace Your Presence brings!

Amen

> *"...mercy [full of glad confidence]*
> *exults victoriously over judgment."*
> James 2:13 AMP

Dear One,

Make sure your heart is strong. Resilience still brings forth the most stamina and is a guard against injury. Minister love and acceptance. Let go of critical judgments. Speak the positive, that builds and renews. Leave behind the critical word that causes others to balk. Simply speak the uplifting truth in love that creates and causes miracles to take place. Be My light bearer. A light bearer does not make judgments, does not criticize. A light bearer brings forth light and radiates with joy, enthusiasm, and love. My light shall overcome the darkness!

Be My Light Bearer!

Your Father

Loving Father,

Thank You, Father, for Your wonderful blessings in my life.

Thank You for causing me to be strong and resilient; teaching me to simply speak the positive, uplifting truth in love, which creates and causes miracles to take place. When I start to make comparisons, please stop me! Help me to always speak the positive, creative word that builds and creates. Father, may I always minister Your love and acceptance with joy and enthusiasm!

Amen

"That you may proclaim the praises of Him who called you out of darkness into His marvelous light."
1 Peter 2:9 NRSV

My Precious One,

Be one of My faithful ones, who hear the call to love and pray, opening the way for My Spirit to move. You are a candle lighter that I use to spark hope, light, joy, and enlightenment into the lives of others. Pray and spend time with Me. Bask in My glory. Build up your spirit through time spent with Me. Partake of My love with exuberance and joy.

Listen To My Heart, My Precious One,

Your Loving Father

Loving Father,

I love being in Your Presence. Thank You, Father, for daily lighting the fire in my heart, as I love and pray and watch Your Spirit move in the most magnificent way. I love You, Father, with all my heart!

Father, Here I am, in Your Presence, to hear Your Words to my heart!

Amen

"Pray at all times (on every occasion, in every season) in the Spirit, with all [manner of] prayer and entreaty."
Ephesians 6:18 AMP

Dear One,

I am your refuge. Secret places of My abiding Presence you shall find as you persistently come into My Presence with devotion. I have carried you in My arms of keeping. I have kept you secluded in the protective place of My love. The Heavens proclaim My glory. I am your protective Father and God. Sweet communion shall be the order of the day, and your heart shall overflow. I am your Lord and your God, and will show you the way to life and liberty.

You Are Precious To Me,

Your Loving Father

Loving Father,

Father, I sit in Your Presence, listening for You to speak to my heart.

It is such sweet communion spending time together with You. You are my Lord and my God; You have shown me the way to life abundant and free, causing my heart to soar on the wings of Your love! Your protective love is always there for me. I love abiding in Your Presence. I love You, Father!

Amen

"Trust in, lean on, rely on, and have confidence in Him at all times, you people; pour out your hearts before Him. God is a refuge for us (a fortress and a high tower)."
Psalm 62:8 AMP

My Child,

Be bold, be strong, be confident. Shine forth My light. Be brave, for your confidence is from Me. I will make you bold. I will make you strong. I will make you brave. I will make you confident in your life. My Presence will become more precious to you as you continue to step out in faith. I will stretch you, and you will grow in grace, truth, and freedom; freedom to think and know My will and My good pleasure in your life. The walls of self-imposed restrictions shall continue to come down, and in their place will be the fragrance and beauty of My heart and My Spirit in your every action and thought. Measure each day by the glory of My Presence.

I Am With You!

Your Loving Father

Loving Father,

Thank You for making me confident and strong; that even as You stretch me, I will grow in grace, truth, and freedom. Father, I am so thankful that the walls in my life shall continue to come down, and in their place will be the fragrance and beauty of Your heart. Thank You, Father, for Your confidence in me. I love You!

Father, Thank You for teaching me to measure each day by the glory of Your Presence.

Amen

"Since we have such [glorious] hope
(such joyful and confident expectation),
we speak very freely and openly and fearlessly."
2 Corinthians 3:12 AMP

Precious One,

Trust in Me. Toss your struggles aside. You are not losing ground. Rest in My ability to accomplish all things. Let go of all worries and struggles. Together we shall overcome and go forth to greater victories. The sky is the limit. Walk in truth and believe. My Word shines so that the clouds disappear. Proclaim My victory in your life. My blessing is upon you. My way of truth always causes the heart to believe.

Trust Me, My Child,

Your Father

Loving Father,

Father, Today I will put all worries aside.

Forgive me for trying to be "good enough"! When I start struggling, I'll know that I'm not resting in Your ability to accomplish and carry through to completion all You've planned for me. Help me to trust in You completely in all things. I love You so much, Father!

Amen

"The sum of Your word is truth;"
Psalm 119:160 AMP

Day 328

Dear One,

My Word to you is freedom in the midst of hardship and pain. Rise above the shadows. Come into My marvelous light, above the clouds and shadows. Be restored in my abundance of joy and freedom of heart. See Me in every moment of every day. Let go of the burdens and cares that would hold you back and steal your joy. Stand strong in My Presence. Abound in the joy of being. I am with you! You are sustained to bless, and to be a blessing. Set into place are the foundation stones in which to build a life of truth, faithfulness, and love!

I Am With You, My Child!

Your Loving Father

Loving Father,

I love the way You bring together the Words from Your heart, and bring beauty into my life. Please fill me with understanding, and bless my life with truth, faithfulness, and love!

Father, Restore Your abundance of joy to my heart!

Amen

"Now the Lord is the Spirit, and where the Spirit of the Lord is, there is liberty (emancipation from bondage, freedom)."
2 Corinthians 3:17 AMP

Day 329

My Beloved One,

Time and time again I have uprooted you and placed you on a new trail, and you have followed with faithfulness in My plan. Now I will do a new thing in your life that shall outshine all the other paths that you have taken. You shall see such beauty on this new journey, and your heart shall rejoice. Bask in the warmth of My smile, and know as never before My ability to continue the preordained and wonderful potential for your life. Change has brought forth the formation of the fruit, and trust has caused it to ripen. Now, the fruit shall bring forth abundance and gladden your heart.

You Are Blessed!

Your Loving Father

Thank You, Father,

Father, You bring such beauty and joy to my life!

For giving me grace to change and adjust in my life as needed. How wonderful to know that seasons of change are Your design for my life. Father, I am thankful for Your Presence in my life. Thank You for touching my heart with Your healing power and for bringing happiness into my days.

Amen

"Say to the righteous that it shall be well with them, for they shall eat the fruit of their deeds."
Isaiah 3:10 AMP

Day 330

Precious One,

Trust in Me. Even when your journey is heavy with concern and despair, look to Me. Restoration of what has been lost is coming your way. The fulfillment is by My Word of promise preordained. See the future unfold. My eyes of love are upon you. Blessings await. Watch them unfold: more blessings than your heart can contain, and My master plan set into motion. Nothing shall close the doors I open for you. Laugh with Me! Set your spirit free. The time has come! You are released to enjoy the abundance intended for your life.

Be Free, My Child, Be Free!

Your Loving Father

Loving Father,

Thank You for lifting the burden of my heart. Thank You for the gift of seeing the future through Your eyes, so that I can be bold as I watch it all unfold. Thank You for the restoration of what has been lost in my life. Your blessings are amazing and my heart is grateful.

Beloved Father, You have never failed me. You are faithful, and I love You!

Amen

"Commit your way to the Lord [roll and repose each care of your load on Him]; trust (lean on, rely on, and be confident) also in Him and He will bring it to pass."
Psalm 37:5 AMP

Day 331

My Dear One,

Time has cleared the way for new beginnings and new opportunities in life. I am your friend and companion on this journey, and it brings Me great pleasure to bless you with good things. Your life has followed many passages of time in growth. As a tree, you have strengthened and become strong. Don't fret with disappointments from your life. The faithfulness you have shown to Me will yield much fruit. You have made many milestones along the way. Let your spirit be refreshed and remember My promises. Many blessings await your life.

You Are Blessed!

Your Loving Father

Loving Father,

Father, Thank You that all the passages of time in my life are safely in Your arms of love.

Please bring peace to my heart and reminders of Your faithful promises. I look to You in all things, knowing that Your guiding hand has always led my life in love and faithfulness. Thank You, Father, that I can trust You. I love You, Father!

Amen

"The fruit of the [uncompromisingly] righteous is a tree of life,"
Proverbs 11:30 AMP

My Precious One,

I will lead you today with delight! Let the fresh breezes of My Spirit brush through your heart and bring happiness to your soul. Your cares will evaporate in the pleasure of My Presence. Recapture the fragrance of joy. Be My faithful child who remains hopeful, and look to Me to bring freedom, laughter, and joy into your life. No good thing do I withhold from My loving, joyful, trusting children.

I Delight In You, My Child!

Your Loving Father

Loving Father,

You bring such delight to my soul! Teach me once again the freedom, laughter, and happiness of recapturing the fragrance of joy in my life. Thank You, Father, that You withhold nothing from me, and I look to You for blessing and guidance every step of each day.

Precious Father, You are the joy and delight of my life!

Amen

*"...delight yourselves in the Lord and
continue to rejoice that you are in Him."*
Philippians 3:1 AMP

My Beloved Child,

My love for you is picture perfect. Green pastures, skies of blue. Soft, trickling streams, be not concerned. My abundant love will see you through. Streams in the desert have watered your soul. They have poured forth refreshing to complete and make you whole. Don't seek to conform or control, but rest and trust in My ability to protect your way. Position yourself in the assurance of My promises. I hear and have heard every word spoken from your heart. Trust in My hand, as I bring you into My plan, complete and blessed.

Love As I Have Loved You,

Your Loving Father

Loving Father,

Father, Speak to my heart.

I am thankful for the wonderful, unexpected blessings of Your love in my life. Thank You for bringing wonderful friends my way, who teach me and invest in my life. Help me to walk daily, in my life, with an attitude of thankfulness. My heart is overwhelmed at the wonder of Your awesome love!

Amen

"It is God himself who has made us what we are and given us new lives from Christ Jesus; and long ages ago he planned that we should spend these lives in helping others."
Ephesians 2:10 TLB

My Beloved One,

Look to Me. When your eyes and heart are open to see, each day is filled with wonder. Lift your heart to Me. The Heavens proclaim the glory of your God. So, too, the earth proclaims the same. Allow Me to transform your life and bring abundance to your heart. Today all things become new. Your destiny awaits!

I Love You, My Precious One!

Your Father

Loving Father,

It is so exciting to see You wherever my eyes look: the dew sparkling like diamonds on the roses; the glory of the brilliance of the sunset that covers the whole sky; double full rainbows of promise across the sky; wispy clouds across the sunset. Truly, everywhere I look, I see the glory of Your Kingdom proclaiming You!

Beloved Father, I am in awe, not only of the beauty of Your love, but of the beauty of Your creation.

Amen

"The Heavens declare the glory of God; and the firmament shows and proclaims His handiwork."
Psalm 19:1 AMP

Day 335

My Precious One,

I have a magnificent plan for your life, a plan predestined by My hand. Before you is the purpose of your life and very being. Seek Me daily, that I might lay out before you the journey as it is intended. The magnitude of all that I have for you is vast. Spend time with Me face to face. Strategic plans I have for you. Listening is the key. You must remember to seek Me in every step. Let your heart be full of hope and peace, love and joy, trusting My plan for your life.

Seek Me Daily, My Precious One,

Your Loving Father

Loving Father,

Precious Father, My heart sings to You with praise, joy, and gladness.

Thank You for filling my heart with hope and trust in You. Father, grant me stamina for the tough days, that I might fulfill Your strategic plan for my life. As I seek You face to face, help me to listen as You speak to my heart.

Amen

"Little children, let us not love [merely] in theory or in speech but in deed and in truth (in practice and in sincerity)."
1 John 3:18 AMP

My Child,

Seek My plan, and stand unmoved by the passing scene. Allow your heart to beat with the strength of My love. Seek to know the strength of My love. And in the fulfillment of that knowledge found, continually search for higher ground. Be alert as you climb that mountain high, as you are tempted to groan and sigh, that every crest and level taken requires trust and faith in Me. You will never be forsaken.

Stand In Faith, My Child,

Your Father

Loving Father,

At times my life journey has seemed long and arduous, but Your hand has been near. Help me to reach out in my life, letting go of past failures and disappointments, reaching for that bright jewel of hope in You. When I am tempted to tire and grow weary—help me to remember that victory requires trust and faith!

Beloved Father, Speak to my heart, I pray, as I walk with You today!

Amen

"And we know that all things work together
for good to those who love God, to those
who are called according to His purpose."
Romans 8:28 NKJV

My Beloved Child,

Sincere praise lifts up the heart into realms of glory—My Presence. My goodness rings and lifts the heavy heart and removes the emptiness. My love is lasting and is made evident through sincere praise and thanksgiving, from a trusting, seeking heart. Search Me out and walk with steadfast abandon. Follow after My ways and find a place of completeness. My ways of faithfulness and love bring forth My beauty upon the earth.

I Love You!

Your Father

Loving Father,

Father, My heart reaches out to You with praise and thankfulness.

It is my desire that my actions would always be pleasing to You and bring joy to Your heart. Help me walk with steadfast confidence. Raise inside my heart, absolute faithfulness that I would serve You with all of my heart. Most of all, I pray that You would cleanse my heart, that I would live freely with a sincere, unfeigned faith!

Amen

"The object and purpose of our instruction and charge is love, which springs from a pure heart and a good (clear) conscience and sincere (unfeigned) faith."
1 Timothy 1:5 AMP

My Precious One,

Strong faith in Me is the key to walking victoriously. Struggles may come, but the strength of My voice commands the enemy to stop; and My triumph in your life is then made evident. Be strong in heart and mind through a firm commitment to listen for and obey that inner witness of My love toward you. Be encouraged this day from the daily distractions that would steal your joy and receive My hand of blessing. My favor is upon you and forever clears the way, as you enter My Presence with praise and thanksgiving. The earth rejoices at the sound of one rejoicing in their King.

We Shall Prevail Together!

Your Loving Father

I Love You, Father,

And rejoice in You with my whole heart! Your gentle, loving voice brings peace to my spirit. Thank You for Your hand of blessing that clears the way before me. I look to You this day and refuse to look to the cares, which would rob my peace. Thank You for Your Presence in my life.

Loving Father, My heart sings to You with such gratefulness and joy.

Amen

"You have given me the capacity to hear and obey."
Psalm 40:6 AMP

Precious One,

Trust in Me always. Though trouble times are near, they will not consume you for My power is greater. I have put you in a safe place surrounded by My love. My love is a shield to you to bring you through to victory. My hand of triumph is in your life. I have commanded it, and it shall come forth. Go forth in faith and trust like a child with a loving, powerful Father, who leads, guides, and protects, saying, "This is the way, walk ye in it." Go forth with freedom, tenacity, and joy. I am with you!

You Are Safe In My Arms!

Your Loving Father

Loving Father,

Father, You are my song in the day and all through the night.

Truly You have put me in a safe place surrounded by Your love. I can trust You completely without hesistation. You have protected my life, shielding me from harm. I can live transparently, with the faith and trust of a child, because I have a loving, powerful Father, who leads and guides and protects me. I love You, Father!

Amen

"Yet the Lord will command His loving kindness in the daytime, and in the night His song shall be with me, a prayer to the God of my life."
Psalm 42:8 AMP

My Precious Child,

Spend time listening and walking, listening and talking, basking in My love and giving it forth with joy. I send you forth this day to play in My Garden of Life, fit and secure in My love. Many will come into this garden with you to share in My love and spend time with you in My Presence, for in My Presence is fullness of joy. In this Garden is every good thing for your development and enhancement—nothing lacking. It is a Garden of hope, for I place within each heart which enters, the knowledge of My love and care, and from that knowledge springs freedom. Linger in My Garden each day. Let Me teach you how to play. For in My Garden, every action and reaction is led by My heart and sets you apart as a precious child of My heart. Through you, I can impart My heart, for you have come apart from the racing, humdrum ways of empty days, into the Garden of My joyful praise.

Your Loving Father

Loving Father,

Nothing in life is more rewarding and wonderful than this lifestyle of listening to You and walking, listening to You and talking, sharing in Your love and giving it forth with joy! I love You, beloved Father!

Father, I am listening intently as You speak to my heart.

Amen

"I am my beloved's [garden] and my beloved is mine!"
Song of Solomon 6:3 AMP

My Precious Child,

Relax and let go of the cares, for My Word shall come through. Continue to wait upon My Word with regularity. Do not let our relationship take second place in your priorities. Come to Me with expectancy, and I will respond. You are My little lamb. Run and jump and play gleefully, being constantly aware of My Presence. Know I am your Shepherd, and obey instantly when I call. Learn to recognize My voice clearly. Practice My Presence continually. Relax, and enjoy My Presence.

I Am Always With You!

Your Loving Father

Loving Father,

I love You, Father! Here I am once again excited to hear Your loving voice and Word to my heart!

It is so true, that as I relax and lay down my care—trusting You to safely carry me through in all things—so much more is accomplished of lasting value. Simply enjoying Your Presence is one of the pure joys of my life. But the greatest joy of life is spending time in Your Presence continually with great expectancy as You speak to my heart!

Amen

"I am the Good Shepherd; and I know and recognize My own, and My own know and recognize Me."
John 10:14 AMP

Day 342

My Precious One,

There is peace in the midst of the storm, as you draw on My love to keep you warm. As you rest in My arms, you will know exactly which direction to go. Don't be fearful. You shall not fail. Your life shall not get off track but will continue moving as I have preordained it for you. You will be fulfilled this side of Heaven. You know in your heart of My promises. Trust is not an issue here. Hope deferred has once again caused weariness to set in. But be encouraged! With Me you know you will win! Release the tendency to rely on others to lift up your heart. Instead, look to Me for My peace and confidence. Let Me be the one you call out to, to receive your strength and peace in all you say and do.

Drink In My Peace!

Your Father

Loving Father,

Forgive me when I reach out to others to give me strength and peace, instead of You! Father, forgive me for allowing weariness to set in, for I do know that Your promises are true and that I shall not fail if I keep my focus on You. It is so comforting to know that as I rest in Your strength, You will lovingly show me exactly which direction to go. I will call out to You, Father, to give me strength and peace, to lift my heart up and cause me to sing. My confidence is in You!

Father, I'm calling out to You today to give me strength and peace, for just a Word from You lifts up my heart and causes me to sing!

Amen

"It is better to trust and take refuge in the Lord than to put confidence in man."
Psalm 118:8 AMP

Day 343

My Child,

I have formed you and brought you to this place of total surrender and grace. You have been patient in this place of pruning and grooming, bringing you forth to this new day of provision and new vision. Your cup shall overflow with new blessings. I have prepared you well. My hand of love is here to guide you, because you are Mine. And now, My precious dove, you shall more fully reflect My love in everything you say and do, which is My perfect will for you.

You Are Precious To Me,

Your Loving Father

Loving Father,

Thank You, Father, for renewed vision in my life.

Continue to form and shape my life. Help me to be patient and lay aside my cares and trust You completely. Thank You, loving Father, for all of the pruning and grooming through the years, by Your hand of love, to help me stand the test of time! I love You, Father!

Amen

"O LORD, You have searched me [thoroughly] and have known me."
Psalm 139:1 AMP

My Precious One,

The scenery is changing, My child, along your pathway chosen by Me. A new path is ahead—a place of beauty, peace, and fellowship with Me. Once again you will come to a new day full of hope and excitement. For now, continue to bathe in the wonderment and beauty of this appointed time of quiet in My Presence. Let Me take care of the rest of your life. It is safe in My hands and shall come forth to your joy and to My glory. Rejoice in the now, in the magnitude and the absolute beauty of all I have created for your life.

I Treasure This Time With You!

Your Loving Father

Loving Father,

I can see You have a plan to bring fulfillment and destiny to my life. Help me to keep my trust in Your capable and loving hands. The times of quiet in Your Presence are times of wonderment, beauty and enjoyment with You. Father, I am so glad that I am on Your pathway, chosen by You!

Father, Thank You for this place of peace.

Amen

"...the wise and their works are in the hands of God."
Ecclesiastes 9:1 AMP

My Child,

Be satisfied with who you are, where you are, and where you are going, knowing that I hold all things in My hands. Your growth is in My hands, and all it requires is a willing and dedicated heart, walking with faith and love. My joy is yours. A joyful heart is a peaceful heart, filled with trust, motivated by a desire to walk in righteousness. Fulfillment and trust walk hand in hand. Trust in My mighty hand to move in your behalf. Have faith.

Trust Me, My Child!

Your Loving Father

Loving Father,

Father, Thank You for the hope and peace You give.

I know I can lean on Your promises with complete trust. I hunger to know You more. As I totally trust You with my life, I know You will bring forth the fulfillment of Your destiny for me in Your time and in Your way. I trust You, Father!

Amen

"Now may the God of hope fill you with all joy
and peace in believing, that you may abound
in hope by the power of the Holy Spirit."
Romans 15:13 NKJV

Dear One

I love you, My child. You are so dear to My heart and bring Me great pleasure. Listen for My Words spoken from My heart to yours. My promises ring clear, proclaiming My love. Struggle not. Simply rest. Spend time in My Presence and receive My breathtaking Words of hope, peace, and joy. Be a reflection of Me, that the world might see and hear with clarity My heart of love for them. Treasure My people as I do. Walk joyfully with a song in your heart.

I Love You, My Child,

Your Loving Father

Loving Father,

No wonder my heart sings with such happiness. My song comes naturally because of Your blessings in my life. Your love is truly breathtaking and fills my life with peace! Father, You have taught me to treasure my life and those You have placed in it. I am so grateful. Help me to remember always every blessing and to be thankful.

Father, My heart is listening for the beautiful Words and music that only You can bring.

Amen

"My heart is fixed, O God, my heart is steadfast and confident! I will sing and make melody."
Psalm 57:7 AMP

My Child,

I charge you this day to know the hearts of those around you. Be sincere and seek to know and love them for who they are. That expression of love will free their lives from fear and doubt. My love will set them free. Be a messenger of My love, joy, freedom, and truth. Restore confidence through Me. Help them to see the potential of their lives in Me. Be a standard of love, freedom, and joy. Every time you hug each one, and smile at each one, you impart these precious elements of My heart. It is all part of My plan.

Love As I Love You!

Your Loving Father

Loving Father,

Father, Who would You have me reach out to this day?

Help me to be filled with compassion for those You have placed in my life. Help me to be sensitive to the hurts and cares of those around me, that I would reach out with tenderness.

Amen

"Freely you have received, freely give."
Matthew 10:8 NKJV

Dear One,

I have surrounded you with My love. My truth will win out in all things, and My compassion shall rule and bind up hurts and fears. Reach out unafraid of repercussions. Reach out and love, and let Me take care of the results. Proceed with love and acceptance for those who feel none. I am with you, My child, to bring healing and wholeness. Let Me lead, and together we shall see transformations take place. Love and joy surround your life at every turn.

Love Heals!

Your Father

Loving Father,

Help me to walk my life out in confidence. Help me to stand secure in Your plan to enjoy each piece as it appears to complete the whole, a continual transformation. I do trust You to bring forth Your restoration and transformation in my life. You have surrounded me with Your love. Thank You for giving me compassion, love, and acceptance for those You have placed in my life. Thank You for Your healing and wholeness!

Father, Thank You for Your transforming power in my life.

Amen

"Show mercy and compassion Everyone to his brother."
Zechariah 7:9 NKJV

Day 349

My Child,

I have set before you a course in life to bring hope and love to many on the trail of hopelessness. Continue to reach out that others would be strengthened and hearts filled with freedom, love, and hope. Continue to lift up weary arms with the promise of spring within their hearts, bringing direction and fulfillment where there was disillusionment and fear. Release unto Me all weariness and weights. My heart for you has always been to walk with Me and win. March forth, dear child of My heart, unencumbered, flying free, following My lead.

You Are Blessed!

Your Loving Father

Loving Father,

Father, I release all weariness and weights to You.

The safety of Your love heals and renews. Thank You, Father, for setting for me a course to bring hope and love to those You have placed in my life.

Amen

"Wait and hope for and expect the Lord;
be brave and of good courage and let
your heart be stout and enduring."
Psalm 27:14 AMP

My Child,

Measure your progress by your peace. Be not in a rush to accomplish all that is set before you. Let the pieces fit together. Don't force them together. You shall see order and discipline descend and take up residence. Let Me bring forth perfection in every way. Your days are all assigned. Take them one at a time with joy. Blessed assurance is yours that much is prepared and shall come to pass. Rise above the seeming indecision and frustration. Rise above the negative aspects, and let My Spirit reign once again in your heart and mind. Be still and know that I am God. Enjoy the quietness and peace that I give. Let the tranquility and beauty of My creation be a soothing, healing ointment to your soul.

Be At Peace, My Child!

Your Father

Thank You, Father,

For reminding me to measure my progress by peace. Such peace comes from knowing that my days are assigned by You. Thank You for the gift of life and joy. I seek to truly and peacefully trust You with confidence.

Loving Father, Your peace is a soothing, healing ointment to my soul.

Amen

"In quietness and in [trusting] confidence shall be your strength."
Isaiah 30:15 AMP

Precious One,

I am with you to bring forth the very best in your life. The strength of My Word never varies. It is immovable and unchangeable. Be at peace and rejoice, for My promises shall come forth unhindered, unhurried, and unyielding. You can set your heart in this. You shall be blessed. Strength of purpose, combined with strength of will, My will, brings forth victory. Be still and know that I am your God. I bring forth that strength and will of purpose.

I Am Always With You!

Your Loving Father

Loving Father,

Father, Thank You for bringing purpose in my life.

Help me to maintain a strong stance of faith. Help me to remember the blessings in my life and to walk my life out in thankfulness. I want to know You more to hear Your voice clearly.

Amen

"Be strong and let your heart take courage, all you who wait for and hope for and expect the Lord!"
Psalm 31:24 AMP

My Child,

My peace is upon you, it is in you, it is through you, and you shall know in ways beyond your understanding how deep that peace runs like a river within you. Your peace will be evident to all who come in contact with you. It is a peace that produces life and cleansing in you, and in those who are near you. There will be a joy in you that is unexplainable. Rest in this peace. Let your life continue to be carried along by that peace.

Remain In My Peace, My Child,

Your Loving Father

Loving Father,

You have patiently led me through the many layers of my life to fully release the potential within. What joy, when that peace is released. Thank You for teaching me to follow Your peace. I love You, Father!

Father, Thank You for leading me by Your peace.

Amen

*"You are a fountain [springing up] in a garden,
a well of living waters, and flowing streams...."*
Song of Solomon 4:15 AMP

My Child,

Be patient and watch for the fulfillment of all your hopes and dreams. Dream big, and have the courage to express all your expectations to Me. I have placed within you hopes and desires—continue to proclaim them without fear. Carry on, dear child of My heart, and you will see great things brought forth by My very own hand, a wonderful part of My master plan. Share with Me every thought, hope, and longing. Be strong and alert, speaking My Word over your life. Pursue Me and time spent in My Presence. I created you to be a masterpiece. So step out with pride, with Me at your side, never missing a beat, as each step we complete together.

Continue Dreaming Big, My Child,

Your Father

Loving Father,

Faithful Father, Thank You that You always have new dreams for me to believe for.

Long ago You began to birth many promises within my heart and the courage to dream big! Your promises still resound in my heart, and I look to You for the fulfillment. Your provision has always been in my life, and I have found safety in Your Presence. You are always faithful to Your Word.

Amen

"Such hope never disappoints or deludes or shames us, for God's love has been poured out in our hearts through the Holy Spirit Who has been given to us."
Romans 5:5 AMP

Day 354

My Precious One,

Blessed, blessed, I say, you are blessed. You are like an untapped spring, waiting to burst forth with abundant life. It brings such pleasure to My heart to bless and enrich your life with good things. Go forth now with confidence and ever-growing faith in My ability to see you through to every victory in every circumstance, and to confirm and make known My full and complete blessings. Together we shall continue to rejoice and see fruit spring forth in every season of your life.

The Blessings Of My Heart Are With You!

Your Loving Father

Wonderful Father,

Every day, walking with You is a treasure in my life. You're teaching me that life holds such beauty, that those who see and hear Your heart never need to fear, for You are always there. Every moment of every day is a gift from You. Everywhere I look I see the gifts given by You. Thank You, Father!

Loving Father, May I always see through Your eyes.

Amen

"Blessed (happy, fortunate, to be envied) are all those who [earnestly] wait for Him, who expect and look and long for Him [for His victory, His favor, His love, His peace, His joy, and His matchless, unbroken companionship]!"
Isaiah 30:18 AMP

Precious One,

Keep your eyes on Me. Listen for the Words of My Spirit. Lift up before Me the cares that would weigh your heart down. Walk in absolute freedom each day. Seek after My love, that you might understand that I am with you at all times. You are blessed because you are My child. You are loved beyond comprehension. Keep your heart free of cares and look to Me. Walk in honesty and walk in truth.

Love As I Love You!

Your Loving Father

Loving Father,

Beloved Father, Thank You for teaching me Your ways.

The joy of my day is when I receive Your Words of encouragement, love, and wisdom to my heart. More and more, the reality of Your love is causing my heart to spring forth with happiness and renewal as I discover the wonderment of all You have in store and recall the things You have done, in and through Your love for me!

Amen

"Blessed are the pure and heart, For they shall see God."
Matthew 5:8 NKJV

My Child,

Seek after Me and be blessed. Walk with a light, sure step. I have fashioned for you a pathway that is abundant with joy and thanksgiving. Blessed assurance is yours, My child, for I have given it to you. You shall know heart peace as few have known—heart rest that shall bring you great happiness. Listen with your whole heart. There is much I have to tell you, much for you to learn and know. The time is now. Open up your heart to receive. Abundant blessings go to the listening heart. No good thing shall be withheld from you. Respond with delight, and I shall respond to you with fullness of joy. Have you not heard? Have you not seen the rewards I have stored up for you? Seek My Kingdom, and all these things shall be added unto you.

Listen With Your Heart, My Child,

Your Loving Father

Wonderful Father,

You are so willing to share Your wisdom and Your heart with me, and yet I spend so much of my time doing other things. Please forgive me for the times when I neglect our precious relationship. I truly want to be like a small child who asks about everything, because Father, You have said to ask, seek, and knock, for anyone who asks, receives, and he who seeks, finds, and the door will be opened to those who knock. There is much You have to tell me, much for me to learn and know. Truly, I come to You seeking.

Loving Father, I have always wanted to ask You about:

Amen

"But seek first the kingdom of God and His righteousness, and all these things shall be added to you."
Matthew 6:33 NKJV

Precious One,

Let your heart overflow with the goodness of My Spirit. Don't think on past sorrows, but look to the immediate future with joy and anticipation. My heart reigns within your heart. Hearken the rising of a brand-new day. Make way for the promise of spring. Await in expectancy for I bring you an uplifted heart, bubbling up with joy and thanksgiving. My abundance is near. Give ear and listen to the coming of My Spirit. Stand strong in the radiance of My smile. I shall lift you up and speak to you My Words of life!

I Delight In You,

Your Loving Father

Loving Father,

Wonderful Father, I am listening with anticipation for Your Words of life.

In even the most difficult times You have been ever near. When I come through a difficult time You have always been there awaiting with wonderful blessings and times of refreshing. You are such a wonderful, loving God! I am so grateful! Truly, my heart is overflowing with the goodness of Your love unto me.

Amen

"Glory in His holy name; let the hearts of those rejoice who seek and require the Lord [as their indispensable necessity]."
Psalm 105:3 AMP

Day 358

My Child,

I have made you stable and secure. Look to Me when you feel faint within your spirit. Look to Me and mount up as upon eagles' wings, and soar once again in the Heavenlies. Don't worry over the details of this life. Leave the cares in My hands. I have them well in hand. I will handle them. Simply walk with freedom, grace, and trust in My ability to see you through each upheaval in the road. Walk renewed with My peace, joy, and protection over you. Be at rest and remember, I am your Creator, the perfector and director of all things pertaining to you. You will not miss out on My best for you. By My power, yours is an abundant life to enjoy.

Fly With Freedom, My Child!

Your Father

Faithful Father,

Thank You for Your peace and for Your blessings in my life. When I am faint and weary, help me remember to look to You. Thank You for reminding me to leave the cares in Your hands and simply walk with freedom, grace, and trust in Your ability to see me through each event of my life. Thank You, Father, for not only increasing my strength, but causing it to multiply and making it to abound!

Father, Right now I am listening for Your voice.

Amen

"He gives power to the faint and weary, and to him who has no might He increases strength [causing it to multiply and making it to abound]."
Isaiah 40:29 AMP

Day 359

My Child,

Make of your heart a resting place. Come often to the well of My renewal to be refreshed and refurbished. Maintain an unruffled spirit. The desires of your heart are the desires of My heart, for I put those desires there. Continue on, rejoicing in life. Nothing shall deter your steps. Be assured, be sustained, and be confident of this very thing, that what I have begun, I shall complete. A storehouse of treasures have I placed in your heart. Continue to feed that storehouse with the treasure of My Word.

Rest In Me,

Your Loving Father

Loving Father,

Father, Thank You for bringing restoration to my heart.

Every day I am more aware of the renewal that You have placed in my heart. Your love delights me with such joy! Thank You, Father, that I can be confident of this very thing, that what You have begun in my life You will complete, beyond my expectations and to Your glory!

Amen

*"I will cry to God Most High, Who performs on
my behalf and rewards me [Who brings to pass
His purposes for me and surely completes them]!"*
Psalm 57:2 AMP

My Child,

You have called upon Me and I have answered your cry. From the beginning of time My plan has been in existence for you. Do not be discouraged in your search and desire to walk in the fullness of My Spirit. But rest knowing I am always near. My strength is yours. Draw on My strength, My wisdom, and My peace through My Word and My Spirit, for they are yours. Walk with Me, and discover the joy and delight of victory!

You Are Victorious In Me!

Your Loving Father

Loving Father,

It's been the journey of a lifetime, and I know it's only begun. I want to know You more and spend time in Your Presence. My heart hungers for You every day. I am listening for Your voice—speak to my heart.

Beloved Father, I am drawing on Your strength and wisdom today.

Amen

"Who has saved us and called us with a holy calling, not according to our works, but according to His own purpose and grace which was given to us in Christ Jesus before time began."
2 Timothy 1:9 NKJV

My Faithful Child,

Look out over the vastness of all that is before you. It is limitless. See, the times and the days, the weeks and the years, are culminating into a time of richness and focused fulfillment and blessing. Continue on in your quest to know My Word. The days ahead are rich and full; full of the knowledge and character of My Word to you. Reach out your heart and mind to receive deeply, and I shall make of you a rich fountain of life—abundant life, in My Name. You shall be refreshed and restored, filled with My glory, peace, faithfulness, and love. It will come upon you and transform you, making of you a servant in whom I am well pleased. Continue on, My child, and know that the door is open wide and the fulfillment is sure. Don't strain to fulfill My dreams in you. Take the land step-by-step.

You Are Precious To Me,

Your Loving Father

Loving Father,

Precious Father, My heart reaches out to You.

Thank You that I shall fulfill Your dreams for me, and for Your refreshment and restoration. Thank You for helping me to know You and Your Word, with understanding by the power of Your Holy Spirit. Strengthen my inner spirit. Thank You for renewing my heart and refreshing my life, in Your Name! I love You, Father!

Amen

"Your Word has revived me and given me life."
Psalm 119:50 AMP

My Faithful Child,

As you continue to know My gifts and blessings for you, your life will become brighter and you will never be lonely again, for I am always there, opening new doors of delight to your heart. Strength of character, fortitude, resilience, and the knowledge of My love and heart are all gifts I have bestowed upon you in abundance. Strength of will, that will to do My will in the face of all obstacles and temptations. Fortitude to stand in the midst of the storm, and resilience to rejoice and sing praise to Me in the midst of the storm. The knowledge of My heart shall increase, and you shall know beyond the shadow of any doubt the abundance of My love. Stand in amazement at what I shall do.

You Have Been Faithful!

Your Loving Father

Precious Father,

I have strengthened my resolve to follow You. Now I see what it really means to be completely carefree. You have been with me in all things—my constant and trusted companion. I am so thankful, Lord, for Your Presence in my life.

Loving Father, My heart reaches out to You.

Amen

"A faithful man shall abound with blessings,"
Proverbs 28:20 AMP

My Precious One,

Be resolute, strong, and secure—for you shall walk confidently. Every decision you make will have tremendous meaning as we go forward and My promises to you shall become the fulfillment of your dreams and wishes. Sure, secure, and sound shall every step be, orchestrated and directed by My heart of love toward you. Your heart will be light and full of happiness, and your praises will ring in exhilaration and joy, pure joy.

Be Happy And Carefree With Me, My Child!

Your Loving Father

Loving Father,

Father, Your love fills my heart.

You have put a new song in my heart, and my happiness sings through my life every moment of every day. It is so precious to know that You love me and that I am treasured by You. You have given my life meaning. Father, my heart is so filled with exhilaration and love for You.

Amen

"And He has put a new song in my mouth,
a song of praise to our God."
Psalm 40:3 AMP

My Child,

Your name is written in My book of life, created by My hand, formed by My love. Each element of your nature was created by My hand and fashioned purposefully. Enjoy each facet of who you are. You are My creation, a delight to Me in every way. I am your loving Father and Creator. I am ever watchful over you. Be confident in each facet of your life, for I preordained your way long ago. You are My creation—a beautiful picture to reflect My love. Precious in My eyes are those who awake to the sound of My voice, to know that everything about them is precious in My sight, part of the reflection of My love. Each facet is to be drawn together in unity to create a symphony of praise.

You Are Formed By My Love,

Your Loving Father

Loving Father,

It's the desire of my heart to awake every morning to the sound of Your voice speaking to my heart. Father, please place a song in my heart each day. I want my whole being to be a symphony of praise to You, reflecting Your love, every moment of every day of my life!

Father, You bring so much joy and music to my heart.

Amen

"...rejoice because your names are written in heaven."
Luke 10:20 NKJV

My Precious Child,

Built within every fiber of your being is the purpose and plan I have designed for your life. Day-by-day it comes forth, many times unheralded and unobserved, but now you shall see your life begin to unfold in brand-new ways. You will clearly see what has been there all along. You have prepared. You have been faithful. You have seen Me in everything. My heart sings for you, My child, for you have heard My voice and yielded to it. The days, the months, and the years are all coming together to form the beautiful song of your life. Mysteries will come to light. Every day becomes a testament of My love for you. As the rising sun over the mountains, this day proclaims My promise and abundance for your life. This is a brand-new day, a time of fresh beginnings. Rejoice and be glad!

I Love You!

Your Father

Loving Father,

I can't imagine not walking daily with You, for every day is a living testament of Your love. Thank You for touching my life with peace and purpose. You are my God and Creator, Lord of the universe. You are my loving Father. Thank You for creating me for intimate friendship and for loving me as Your most precious and valuable creation. Thank You, Father, for Your love!

Precious and Beloved Father, You are my heart's desire. I will always cherish each living moment of every day with You, as You speak to my heart!

Amen

"O come, let us sing to the Lord; let us make a joyful noise to the Rock of our salvation! Let us come before His presence with thanksgiving; let us make a joyful noise to Him with songs of praise!"
Psalm 95:1-2 AMP

My Personal Moments with God

My Personal Moments with God

My Personal Moments with God

My Personal Moments with God

My Personal Moments with God

My Personal Moments with God

My Personal Moments with God

Rosalie Willis began journaling more than 30 years ago in an effort to draw closer to God, which was the inspiration for this book—conceived as a way to acquaint readers with the very personal side of God's love.

Rosalie is the founder and co-director of *A Company of Women International*, a family of women's ministries coming together in the unity of God's love. An important part of *A Company of Women* is *PraiseNet*, an International Prayer Network, through which all can pray together regarding needs, and rejoice in shared victories, while connecting hearts around the world.

Also a musician, Willis has written and recorded music to all 150 Psalms, word for word from the Amplified Version of the Bible. Most recently Willis released her first CD, *The Psalms*, which includes 12 complete chapters from the Psalms.

Rosalie currently has three other titles in the marketplace; *A Walk With Jesus*, *Walking On With Jesus*, and *The Singing Bride*.

Frequently speaking at retreats and conferences, Rosalie has a true devotion in life to encourage others in their pursuit toward a personal and intimate relationship with God. For additional information on seminars, scheduling speaking engagements, or to write the author, please address your correspondence to:

Rosalie Willis
P.O. Box 324
Post Falls, Idaho 83877-0324

e-mail: praise@imbris.com

www.rosaliewillis.com

www.acompanyofwomen.org

Additional copies of this book and other titles by Rosalie Willis
are available from your local bookstore.

If this book has touched your life, we would love to hear from you.

Please write us at:

White Stone Books
Department E
P.O. Box 2835
Lakeland, Florida 33806

Or visit our website at:
www.whitestonebooks.com

"...To him who overcomes, I will give some of the hidden manna to eat.
I will also give him a white stone with a new name written on it,
known only to him who receives it."

Revelation 2:17

WHITE STONE BOOKS
LAKELAND, FLORIDA